KEY SKILLS
LEVEL 1

INFORMATION TECHNOLOGY, APPLICATION
OF NUMBER AND COMMUNICATION

R.P. Richards

Published by

PAYNE-GALLWAY
P U B L I S H E R S L T D

26-28 Northgate Street, Ipswich IP1 3DB
Tel: 01473 251097 • Fax: 01473 232758

www.payne-gallway.co.uk

Acknowledgements

I must thank Pat and Oliver at Payne-Gallway for their help and support in producing this book.

I am also grateful to Bernard Harrison for his helpful comments and suggestions.

Illustrations © Veronica Ward,
In Words & Pictures

Cover picture:
© 'The Ancients' by Chris Chapman
www.chrischapmanart.com
email: chris@chrischapmanart.com

First edition 2002

10 9 8 7 6 5 4 3 2 1

A catalogue entry for this book is available from the British Library.

ISBN 1 903112 51 6

Copyright © R.P. Richards 2002

Design and artwork by:
Direction Advertising and Design Ltd.
www.direction-advertising.com

Printed in Great Britain by
W.M. Print, Walsall, West Midlands

Preface

Who is this book for?

This book aims to provide teachers and students with the basic information required to become proficient in the skills identified in the QCA specifications for Information Technology, Application of Number and Communication Key Skills at Level 1.

What is the purpose of the book?

The author interprets the key skills specifications in a practical, hands-on way, leaving both teachers and students in no doubt as to what is required for both the Key Skills portfolio and the externally-set tests.

The knowledge and skills are presented in short sections in a straightforward, step-by-step manner. Lots of examples are given, followed by suggestions for class exercises or discussion. Each chapter includes a sample assignment similar to those the teacher should provide the student with in order to produce evidence for their portfolio. These assignments give a contextual setting, a list of tasks and details of what evidence should be collected. A table then relates the assignment tasks to the QCA specifications. The next section in each chapter signposts other Key Skills that may be covered whilst completing the assignment tasks. This is followed by a list of ideas for other similar, assignments. Finally each chapter includes a set of sample test questions, similar to those the student is likely to encounter in the external assessment.

Extra web site resources

Extra resources are provided on the Payne-Gallway web site.

www.payne-gallway.co.uk/ks

These include answers to all of the exercises, sample assignments and sample test questions in each chapter. The sample documents provided in Appendix B can also be downloaded.

For additional teachers' resources follow the link from
www.payne-gallway.co.uk.
For example, you can download the Overhead Transparency Masters which are provided to accompany each of the chapters in this book. They are for use by teachers to summarise the underpinning knowledge required.

Contents

Introduction - For Teachers

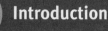

The Key Skills units

The QCA specifications for the Key Skills units in Information Technology, Application of Number and Communication at Level 1 are shown in Appendix A.

Each unit comprises three sections:

Part A explains what the student needs to know.

Part B identifies what the student must do.

Part C provides examples of the activities through which skills might be developed.

Assessment

Students will be assessed through portfolio evidence (described in Part B above) for each of the three Key Skills units. When the portfolio of evidence has been assessed (and possibly moderated by the awarding body) the student will receive a Key Skills certificate for each Key Skill unit.

These Key Skills units are also assessed by external assessment (a test of the skills identified in Part A above.) Students will receive a Key Skills certificate for each successful external assessment.

Preparing for the test

All of the tests at Level 1 are of 1 hour duration and comprise 40 multiple-choice questions. The questions will be based around a number of common themes linked to common, everyday situations.

Ensure that the students have covered the skills and knowledge in all the chapters of this book. Even if they do not intend to use similar activities as evidence in their portfolio, they could be asked a question on them in the test. They should complete the sample assignment at the end of each chapter. They should also attempt the sample test questions associated with each chapter. When they have covered all the topics they should attempt the sample tests available from the QCA web site (www.qca.org.uk), which will provide further practice in the type of questions they are likely to encounter. The tests that they take as part of the assessment for the Key Skills qualification will be externally set by QCA. They are designed to enable students to show what they know and how they can apply the knowledge they have gained to an appropriate task. It is likely that the awarding body will offer more than one opportunity during the year for the students to sit the test. The school or college will notify the students of the date(s).

The Portfolio

Students should work through each chapter of this book and complete each sample assignment. This will ensure that they have covered all of the skills required for section B of the specification. They then need to complete a similar assignment to provide the evidence required for their portfolio. It is important to note that for each evidence component specified in section B, all the bullet points must be met within the same activity and not 'ticked off' individually. Also, all assignment briefs or tasks (which should be as relevant to the candidate as possible) should be included with each piece of portfolio evidence.

Many tasks that are assessed for portfolio work could be used in more than one Key Skill assessment so a methodical filing system is essential. A ring binder or box file with three dividers, one for each Key Skill, would be a minimum - this will probably become one for each unit in due course as the student progresses through the various Key Skills levels.

The production of the portfolio for internal assessment in any Key Skills unit should not be perceived by the student as containing only the successful conclusion of a project or topic. It is not about just this finished product. It is about showing all the steps along the way and proving that the student has made corrections to produce the finished product. From the beginning students should keep notes of discussions and meetings either internal to the school or college or from external sources.

They should be encouraged to make preliminary sketches, plans and drafts of tasks they do, and ensure that these are also safely filed, as they will be needed to provide evidence of the development of a project or task.

Logging the evidence

It is important that students index or reference their portfolio. Each piece of work should be given a unique number - this can then be cross-referenced between key skills. The student should be given some form of log book (a sample is shown in Appendix B – it is not so much a 'book' as a collection of sheets to complete and put in the portfolio). This allows the student to record the context of evidence that they have generated and its exact location in their folder. It should also record the date the work was assessed and by whom.

Every time a student produces a piece of work for their Key Skills portfolio they should:

- put the piece of work into their portfolio and number it (e.g. in the top right-hand corner).

- find the appropriate **KEY SKILLS LOG BOOK COMPONENT SHEET** (e.g. Component IT1.1, etc.). Fill in the column **HOW MET** against the appropriate Assessment Criteria (bullet point) and Purpose. (Students can use the paragraph **Relating this chapter to the specification** near the end of the appropriate chapter to help them to do this.)

- date it and ask the assessor to sign it.

- in their **KEY SKILLS LOG BOOK UNIT SUMMARY** record the number they have assigned to the piece of work against the appropriate Key Skills requirement.

Additional web site resources

Visit **www.payne-gallway.co.uk/ks** for additional resources to accompany this book. The forms in Appendix B can be downloaded for your use.

Chapter 1
Introducing the Case Study

The Broomhill Sports Club

Many of the exercises in this book are based around the Broomhill Sports Club. It assumes that you, the reader, are a student who applies successfully for a part-time job at the club. You will learn and practise the key skills in IT, Communication and Number by completing tasks associated with your employment.

You can get some idea of the facilities that the club has to offer by reading their advertising leaflet shown on the following page.

 Class Discussion

List some of the administrative tasks that you think need to be done to maintain the success of the Broomhill Sports Club.

In which of these tasks would a computer help the staff?

 Class Discussion

What tasks might staff have to carry out that would involve them in reading numerical information from tables or charts?

What tasks might staff carry out that require them to record measurements?

What tasks might staff carry out that require them to perform calculations?

 **Class Discussion**

List some of the situations that might occur at the Sports Club where good verbal communication would be important for the staff.

List some of the situations that might occur at the Sports Club where good written communication would be important for the staff.

List some of the instances where you think it would be necessary for staff to be able to find out information from written sources.

A990 FROM CHELMSFORD
THE CROWN PH
B123 FROM BRENTWOOD
FAIRWAY ROAD
HIGH STREET
MAJORS CORNER
P
MANLEY ST
HALE ROAD
BROOMHILL
SPORTS CLUB

BROOMHILL
SPORTS CLUB

BROOMHILL
SPORTS CLUB

FITNESS FOR ALL

Fitness for all

Get in shape with us!

A new approach to a healthy lifestyle

We offer you more than you expect:

- A choice of over 30 activities
- Trained instructors available
- All inclusive membership or 'pay as you go'
- Luxury changing facilities
- Free members magazine
- Health and beauty
- All facilities and services FREE to members

Why not come along and try out our facilities on a 'pay as you go' basis first?

SWIMMING
Our 20m swimming pool has allocated speed lanes at all times.
Adults:
£1.80 per hour
Children:
£1.10 per hour

ARCHERY
Why not try archery lessons with our qualified instructor?
Tues and Thurs:
10.00 - 11.00am
£3.50 per person
Must be booked in advance.

FOOTBALL
Football is not just for the men - we have women and girls' teams as well as boys and men competing in local leagues at all levels. Ask reception for details.

SQUASH
Book one of our three squash courts and join the squash 'ladder'.
£3.50 per court, per hour.

AEROBICS
Our aerobic classes are very popular - work out with your friends.
Every morning
9.30 - 10.30am
£2.50 per person.

TENNIS
Broomhill boasts two indoor courts in addition to four outdoor ones.
£2.50 per person per court

GYMNASIUM
We have a fully equipped gymnasium with all of the latest equipment.
£2.50 per hour
Over 16s only.

OTHER SPORTS
Many other activities are available including basketball, badminton and table tennis.

All activities Free to members

We'll help you achieve a better lifestyle. Look better! Feel better! Work better! Sleep better!

MEMBERSHIP FEES

	One person	Joint membership	Family membership
Full membership	£250	£350	£400
Swimming only	£100	£150	£200
Gymnasium only	£125	£175	N/A
Sauna and sunbed	£75	£125	£150

OPENING TIMES

Monday	7.00am - 10.00pm
Tuesday	7.00am - 10.00pm
Wednesday	6.30am - 10.30pm
Thursday	6.30am - 10.30pm
Friday	7.00am - 10.00pm
Saturday	7.00am - 10.00pm
Sunday	7.30am - 9.30pm

Call
09034 222111
to arrange a visit now!

Part 1

Information Technology

1

Chapter 2
Finding & Selecting Information

Sources of Information

An important part of the IT Key Skills qualification is to be able to find different types of information. For example, you may need to find the temperatures for a particular city over a period of time for a spreadsheet, or you may need to collect together some information to compile a newsletter.

There are many places where you can find information and many different ways of finding it.

The main sources of information that we will look at in this chapter are the Internet and CD-ROMs. However to complete some of the tasks for your Key Skills qualification you may well use non-IT sources such as people, books, newspapers and magazines.

The Internet

The Internet is a vast system that connects people and information through computers. By using the Internet you can look up information on any subject you can imagine.

The **World Wide Web (WWW)** has been developed to make it easy for anyone to access and view documents that are stored on computers anywhere on the Internet.

Web Sites are the pages you visit as you travel around the WWW. Every web site consists of one or more documents called pages. An important feature of **web pages** is their ability to contain **hyperlinks**. These are links to another page or location on the WWW. Both text and graphics can be set up as hyperlinks.
A home page is the first page of a web site that the user sees. It serves as an introduction to the web site.

Figure 2.1: The BBC Home page

Every page has its own unique name or address, called a **Uniform Resource Locator (URL)**. When you type a URL it is important that you type it with every dot, slash and colon in the right place.

Figure 2.2: A Uniform Resource Locator (URL)

A **web browser** is a software package you use to view information from the Internet. A browser program, like Internet Explorer or Netscape Navigator, acts as a go-between for your computer and the WWW.

Accessing a known web site

A friend or teacher might recommend a site that you should look at, or you might see one advertised in a magazine or on television.

▶ Start Internet Explorer by clicking the icon on the Quick Launch toolbar (next to the Windows **Start** button). Alternatively, select it from the Programs list on the **Start** menu.

▶ You may be asked if you wish to connect to the Internet. Click **Yes**.

▶ Click inside the address box.

▶ When the URL in the address box appears highlighted, type the web site address, for example *www.bbc.co.uk*. (The *http://* is put in for you.)

▶ Click the **Go** button.

After a few seconds the BBC home page appears on your screen.

▶ Move your pointer around the text and graphics on the BBC home page. The mouse arrow changes to the shape of a hand as it passes over hyperlinks on the page. Usually hyperlinks appear as underlined coloured text or graphics. (The default is to display text links in blue before they are clicked. As soon as they are clicked they change to purple.)

▶ Click on the **News** category. A new page will appear in seconds.

▶ To return to the previous page you can click the **Back** button. (Each time you click the **Back** or **Forward** button on the Internet Explorer toolbar, you are returned to the page you viewed previously during your current browsing session.)

Searching for information

There are plenty of search tools available to help you find the pages you want on the WWW. These tools all work in roughly the same way: you form a search query made up of a keyword or phrase, and the search tool looks through its database of documents on the Internet. It then returns a list of documents that match. Each match is called a hit and contains a hyperlink to the corresponding web page.

There are several different types of search tool – the ones you are likely to use most are **search engines**.

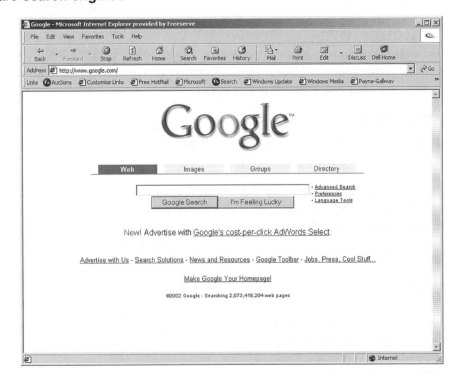

Figure 2.3: The Google search engine

You must take some care in setting up your search query to communicate exactly what you want to find. Remember these useful tips:

- If possible do not use connecting words like *the* and *an*.

- Check your spelling.

- Be specific.

- Try a few different word combinations.

- Run your search using at least two different search tools.

Storing information

Once you have found the exact page you have been looking for you may want to print the page or copy part of the information and save it.

Printing a web page

Printing from Internet Explorer is very similar to printing from other Windows programs such as Word. Clicking the **Print** button on the Standard toolbar sends the page you can see on the screen to the printer. For more control over various options, use the **Print** command from the **File** menu.

To copy and save selected parts of a web page

The easiest way to do this is to copy the text from the web page in Internet Explorer and paste into a new Word document.

- Open a new document in Word.

- Open Internet Explorer, connect to the Internet, and find the web page you want.

- Select the text on the web page and click **Copy** from the **Edit** menu.

- Click on the new Word document on the task bar to bring it onto the screen.

- Click **Paste** from the **Edit** menu.

- Save the new Word document and disconnect from the Internet. (You can do this by right-clicking the Dial-up icon at the bottom right of your screen and selecting **Disconnect**.)

Exercise 1: Log on to a search engine and search for information about the town in which you live. Make a note of the types of sites the search finds for you. Now run the same search on a different search engine and note any different sites it finds.

CD-ROM (Compact Disk Read Only Memory)

CD-ROMs may carry text, pictures, sound, animation and video. These disks can store large amounts of information. For example, encyclopaedias like Encyclopaedia Britannica and Encarta are now available on CD-ROM.

Searches can be made to find specific information and the results displayed, not only in text but also in picture and sound form. There is no interactive capability with these disks, but they do help to visualise a topic and offer examples of distinctive sounds.

Installing a CD-ROM is very simple. Most automatically run a Setup program when you insert them into the CD-ROM drive. If this does not happen do the following:

▶ From the Windows **Start** menu, click on **Run**.

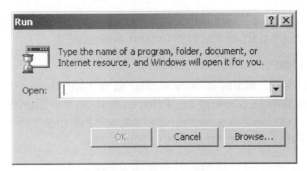

Figure 2.4: Running a program

▶ In the **Run** dialogue box, click on **Browse** to find the CD-ROM drive (often D: or E:) and click on the Setup file for the program.

The Setup program will guide you through the installation.

When you come to run the program, you will find that the CD-ROM must be inserted in the drive as all the reference files are not installed on your computer.

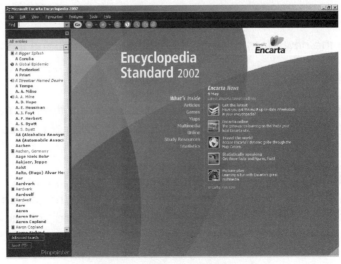

Figure 2.5: Encarta 2002

Tip:
You will see instructions on the screen to guide you round the program and show you, for example, where to enter a search.

E-mail

An easy way to exchange information is electronic mail or e-mail. It can be sent over the Internet to anybody who has an e-mail address.

E-mail addresses are quite like web site addresses and made up in much the same way. The format is always:

username@domain_name

Here username is you and domain_name is either the Internet Service Provider (ISP) who gives access to the Internet, or a web site address.

So, the e-mail address of Pete Grey (Manager of the Broomhill Sports Club) might look like any of these:

petegrey@compuserve.com

pgrey@aol.com

pete@broomhill.demon.co.uk

An e-mail address has no spaces and is usually all in small letters. It must be entered correctly or the message will come back undelivered. Every e-mail address is unique.

Different types of e-mail

There are two types of e-mail. The first is the type you are given when you sign up with an ISP (such as **Freeserve, AOL** or **CompuServe**). To use this type of account you need a special program that allows you to connect to the Internet and collect your mail. One of the most popular ones is Outlook Express, which is supplied with the latest versions of Windows.

The second type of e-mail is called **webmail.** Instead of using a separate program to read and write your messages, you sign up for a free account with a web site. You then have to log on to the Internet for all your e-mailing. One great advantage of webmail is that you can pick up your e-mails from any computer connected to the Internet. Examples of webmail include **hotmail** and **yahoo**.

Advantages of communicating by e-mail

- ❗ It arrives almost instantaneously anywhere in the world.
- ❗ You can attach documents to the e-mail.
- ❗ You can send the e-mail to more than one person at the same time.
- ❗ It is relatively cheap.
- ❗ It is secure and private.

Exercise 2: What disadvantages of e-mail can you think of?

Tip:
Pronounce this as "pete at broomhill dot demon dot co dot uk".

Sample Assignment

Background

Broomhill is one of a chain of Sports Clubs around the country. The company are considering opening a new club in your hometown. You have been asked to do some market research for them on the facilities that already exist in your locality.

Tasks

1   Use several different search engines to find information about six Sports Clubs (or similar facilities) in your local area. Make a note of the results each search engine finds.

2   For each of the six clubs, find out if they have the following:

- A swimming pool – what size is it?

- A Jacuzzi?

- A gym – with what type of equipment?

- Eating facilities e.g. cafe, restaurant etc.?

- Personal trainers?

3   Visit the site **www.multimap.com** and make a map of your local area. Mark on the map (by hand) the location of the six clubs.

4   Choose which club you think is best and save some information about it from one of the web sites you found in task 1. Save the information to disk and print it out.

5   Use a reference CD-ROM to find some information on Jacuzzis.

Evidence to collect

- Notes for task 1.

- Answers to task 2.

- The map you produced for task 3.

- A screenshot of Windows Explorer showing where you saved the file for task 4.

- A printout for task 4.

- A printout of the information found for task 5.

Tip:

To take a screenshot press the **Print Screen** (Prt Scr) button on the keyboard. Open a new Word document and click **Paste** on the **Edit** menu.

Relating the assignment to the specification

Specification Reference (Part B)	What has been done to satisfy this
IT1.1	
• Find and select relevant information.	• Tasks 1, 2 and 5
• Enter and bring in information, using formats that help development.	• Task 3
• Explore and develop information to meet your purpose.	• Task 3
IT1.2	
• Use appropriate layouts for presenting information in a consistent way.	
• Develop the presentation so that it is accurate, clear and meets your purpose.	
• Save information so that it can be found easily.	• Task 4

Other key skills signposting

Communication C1.2 and C1.3

Ideas for other assignments

! Using a reference CD-ROM or the Internet to find out information for your main area of study.

! Using the Internet to look up rail, bus and air timetables to find out the quickest or cheapest way to travel between two towns in this country.

! Using a CD-ROM or the Internet to find pictures for a project.

Sample test questions

1   A multinational organisation has offices in several countries in Europe. They need to send an urgent message to the senior managers in each office. The easiest way to get the message to them would be to:
    A   send it by first class post
    B   send it by motorbike courier
    C   send an e-mail
    D   telephone them

2   A football club needs to add postcodes to the records of its season ticket holders. To do this it uses a national database of postcode information held:
    A   in a card index
    B   in a printed directory
    C   on floppy disk
    D   on CD-ROM

3   To provide instant information to season ticket holders, the football club could:
    A   advertise in the local free newspaper
    B   set up a web site
    C   put up a poster in the town
    D   deliver leaflets to their homes

4   The data used to create the weather forecast should be obtained from:
    A   experiments by school children
    B   automatic weather stations and satellites
    C   tables of information in a reference book
    D   published weather statistics on CD-ROM

5   You are asked to find out about the Tate Modern art gallery in London. Which IT source is most likely to provide this information?
    A   a floppy disk
    B   Internet
    C   scanner
    D   newspaper

6   What tool would be best to search for this information about the Tate Modern?
    A   a search engine
    B   a zip drive
    C   Windows Explorer
    D   a spreadsheet program

7   Which of these is an example of a web browser?
    A   Microsoft Paint
    B   a word-processing package
    C   Google
    D   Internet Explorer

Chapter 3
Working Safely

Introduction

Every organisation has rules about the way it operates. These may not be formal rules and regulations that are written down – they may just be ways of working that all members of staff have got used to following.

Managing your work

Working with files

Almost all of the work that is created using a computer is stored in a file. These files are stored in folders, often on the hard drive of your computer (or on a floppy disk or a company, school or college network). Every file is given a name and it is important that you use sensible filenames that remind you of the contents. Once you are in the workplace the files that are created and stored belong to the organisation. This means that other people may need to be able to find your files, so a well-organised file structure is important.

My Documents is a desktop folder that provides you with a convenient place to store files you want to access quickly. On your desktop it is represented by a folder with a sheet of paper in it. You can create your own subfolders within My Documents, making a simple path to where their files are stored. Remember to save your work regularly.

Working with floppy disks

If you save your work onto a floppy disk, there are a few points to remember.

- The disk must be formatted beforehand – most floppy disks that you buy are already formatted. Formatting means checking the disk for any errors and setting it up to accept data.

- Label the disk clearly and do not lend it to anyone else.

- Store it safely, away from direct sunlight, liquids and magnetic fields.

- Use the write-protect tab at the bottom of the disk so that your work will not be deleted or overwritten.

Figure 3.1:
Write-protecting
a floppy disk

Push the tab down to
lock the disk and up
to unlock.

Chapter 3
Working Safely

Fault logging

Many problems can arise when working with ICT systems. Often the 'faults' are not problems with the system so much as the users not fully understanding how to operate the software, or what messages mean. This is why user training and good documentation are vital to the success of a new ICT system.

Real faults can be sorted out quicker if clear and exact information is passed on to the technical people supporting the system. When reporting a fault the following information should be provided:

! What happened when the fault occurred. If there is an error message, you should tell the technicians exactly what appears on the screen.

! What happened immediately before the fault occurred.

! Details of the equipment and where it is situated.

A fault log should always be kept near to a PC and all details of the problem entered neatly. These records can help to identify equipment that has a recurring fault and provide information on how the fault has been fixed in the past.

Tip:

A recurring fault is one that keeps happening time and time again.

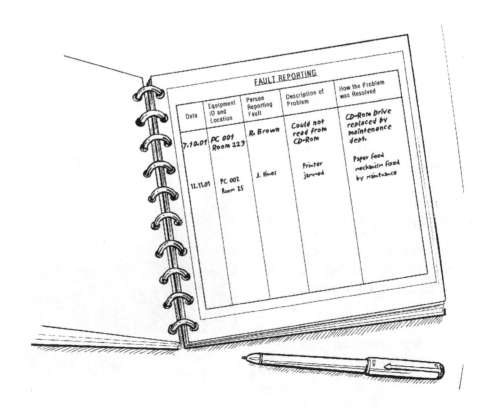

FAULT REPORTING

Date	Equipment ID and Location	Person Reporting Fault	Description of Problem	How the Problem was Resolved
7.10.01	PC 001 Room 223	R. Brown	Could not read from CD-Rom	CD-Rom Drive replaced by maintenance dept.
12.11.01	PC 002 Room 25	J. Hines	Printer jammed	Paper feed mechanism fixed by maintenance

Help systems

If you are not sure how to operate the software or you do not understand an error message, you should make sure you know how to use the Help system provided. All Windows applications have similar Help systems. Follow the instructions below to load the Word Help system:

Note: If you haven't used Microsoft Word before, you might prefer to wait until you have completed Chapter 4 before you try this.

▶ With a Word document open on your screen, select **Help**, **Microsoft Word Help**.

▶ Click on the **Answer Wizard** tab.

▶ Type your question in the **What would you like to do?** box.

▶ Click on **Search**.

A list of topics will be displayed in the left window.

▶ Click on the topic which most closely describes what you want to do.

The help information will appear in the right-hand window.

▶ You can click on the text in blue to take you to more detailed information.

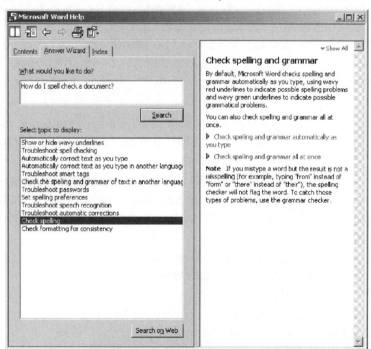

Figure 3.2: The Word Help system

Most Microsoft programs have similar Help systems - take a look at Excel Help too.

Keeping information secure

Computer systems must be controlled to ensure that only authorised personnel have access to data. There are a number of ways in which this can be achieved:

Passwords

Most networks require a user to log on with their password before they can gain access to the computer system. Additional passwords may be required to gain access to certain programs and data. It is important that you do not tell other people these passwords and it is recommended that passwords are frequently changed. In fact many systems are set up to automatically prompt you after a set number of days to change your password.

Virus checks

Viruses are generally developed with a definite intention to cause damage to computer files or, at the very least, cause inconvenience and annoyance to computer users. They are often sent as attachments to e-mails.

Virus checkers need to be installed on all computer systems so that they automatically check for any infected data when the computer is started up. Manual checkers can also be used to check for viruses on floppy disks.

Backup systems

Routine backups of the computer system should be made so that, in the case of serious emergency, the system can be recreated to the last full backup. They are made on a daily, weekly or monthly basis depending on the importance of the data to be backed up. The backup media (magnetic tape, CD-ROM, Zip drive, floppy disk etc.) must be clearly labelled and should be stored in a fire-proof safe, or better still on a different site, so that should a disaster or emergency occur, the backup media will be safe.

Copyright

Computer software is copyright material – that means it is protected in the UK by the Copyright, Designs and Patents Act 1988. It is owned by the software producer and it is illegal to make unauthorised copies.

When you buy software it is often supplied in a sealed package (e.g. CD-ROM case) on which the terms and conditions of sale are printed. This is called the **software licence** and when the user opens the package they are agreeing to abide by the licence terms.

It is illegal to make copies of the software, except for backup purposes, so you are breaking the law if you copy some software from a friend to use on your own computer.

Also be careful about using pictures you find on the Internet. These images may be copyright and belong to the artist or photographer.

Computers and health

Computers can be held responsible for lots of **health problems**, from eyestrain to wrist injuries and back problems.

Figure 3.3: Stress at work

Stress

Stress is often a major factor in work-related illness. Simply thinking about computers is enough to cause stress in some people. It is stressful to be asked to perform tasks which are new to you and which you are not sure you can cope with. It is stressful to know that you have more work to do than you can finish in the time available. It is stressful, even, to have too little to do and to be bored all day.

Repetitive Strain Injury (RSI)

RSI is the name for a variety of disorders affecting the upper body. It can result in numbness or tingling in the arms and hands, aching and stiffness in the arms, neck and shoulders, and an inability to lift or grip objects.

Eyestrain

Computer users are prone to eyestrain from spending long hours in front of a screen. Many computer users prefer a dim light to achieve better screen contrast, but this makes it difficult to read documents on the desk. A small spotlight focussed on the desktop can be helpful. There is no evidence that computer use causes permanent damage to the eyes, but glare, improper lighting, improperly-corrected vision (through not wearing the correct prescription glasses), poor work practices and poorly-designed workstations all contribute to temporary eyestrain.

Computers, health and the law

Employers must conform to certain laws that aim to protect the health of employees working with IT systems.

Employers are required to:

- **!** Check the IT equipment regularly for anything that might affect the health or safety of their employees.

- **!** Provide training to employees in the use of the IT equipment.

- **!** Ensure employees take regular breaks or have changes in activity.

- **!** Provide regular eye tests for workstation users and pay for glasses.

Employees have a responsibility to:

- **!** Use workstations and equipment correctly, in accordance with training provided by employers.

- **!** Bring problems to the attention of their employer immediately and co-operate in the correction of these problems.

Manufacturers are required to ensure that their products comply with these rules. For example, screens must tilt and swivel and keyboards must be separate and moveable. Notebook PCs are not suitable for entering large amounts of data.

Screen must **tilt....**

and **swivel**

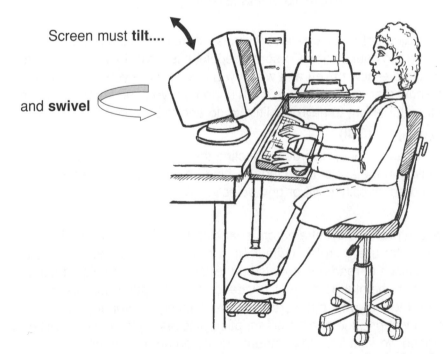

Figure 3.4: Workstations must be ergonomically designed

The working environment

Employers must check:

! Lighting. The office should be well lit. Computers should neither face windows nor back onto a window so that the users have to sit with the sun in their eyes. Adjustable blinds should be provided.

! Furniture. Chairs should be of adjustable height, with a backrest which tilts to support the user at work and at rest, and should swivel on a five-point base. It should be at the correct height relative to a keyboard on the desk.

! Cabling. No cables should lie across the surface of the floor where people can trip over them. They should be under the floor, above the ceiling or housed in trunking.

! Noise. Noisy printers, for example, should either be given covers to reduce the noise or located in a different room.

! Hardware. The screen must tilt and swivel and be flicker-free, the keyboard must be separately attached.

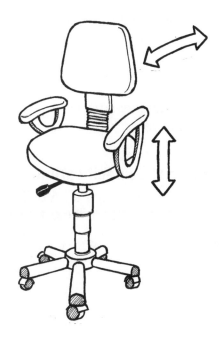

Exercise 1: Is the chair you use at the computer adjustable?

Chapter 3
Working Safely

Sample Assignment

Background

You are asked to conduct a feasibility study into converting your computer room into an office which will employ a number of people working on computers during office hours every weekday.

Tasks

1   Look at the computer equipment in the room.
    Make notes on whether you feel the workstations meet legal requirements. What changes would you suggest?

2   Think about the lighting in the room, would it be suitable for employees working in the office all day?

3   Is the cabling neat and tidy, could it be improved in any way?

4   Is the furniture suitable for office employees? If not, why not?

5   What about the level of noise in and around the room – would it be acceptable?

6   What kind of problems could employees who work all day on computers suffer from?

7   What else can employers do to protect the health of employees working on computers?

Evidence to collect

● A neatly presented report (either hand-written or word-processed) covering the answers to the tasks above.

Relating the assignment to the specification

The information in this chapter is required for Part A of the specification. Students are likely to be assessed on this knowledge in the externally-set test.

Other key skills signposting

Communication C1.3

Sample test questions

1 Cables used to connect computers should be:

    A   lying across the floor

    B   running across the top of the desks

    C   placed in channels under the floor or in the ceiling

    D   frayed at the ends

2 When copying and using a picture from the Internet, it is important to:

    A   give it a new title

    B   keep backup copies of the picture

    C   check who owns the copyright

    D   not mention the source of the information

3 For health and safety reasons, a computer screen should be:

    A   multicoloured

    B   square

    C   capable of swivelling and tilting

    D   easy to move

4 What type of health problem can be caused by using a keyboard or mouse for long periods without a break?

    A   repetitive strain injury (RSI)

    B   low blood pressure (LBP)

    C   skin infection virus (SIV)

    D   visual balance problem (VBP)

5 To save a document for the first time, you have to give it a:

    A   date

    B   two-letter prefix

    C   number in the index

    D   sensible filename

6 Important data on a floppy disk can be protected from being deleted by:

    A   hiding the disk

    B   write-protecting the disk

    C   formatting the disk

    D   using a large label

7 To avoid losing data, a spreadsheet should be regularly:

    A   checked

    B   reorganised

    C   compressed

    D   backed up

Chapter 3
Working Safely

8 A new set of sales results is produced by a company every month. Each month, the sales results should be saved:

A   overwriting last month's results

B   in a new format

C   with a new filename

D   in a graphics package

9 A company has a major fire and the computers are damaged beyond repair. They have lost all their data. What precaution should they have taken?

A   kept backup copies on a different site

B   used sensible filenames

C   kept backup copies of files in the drawer of the computer desk

D   saved the files in separate folders

10 If a program is copyright:

A   you cannot use it

B   you must not make unauthorised copies

C   you can make as many copies as you like

D   it has a recurring fault

Chapter 4
Word Processing

Word Processing is the use of computers to produce documents which contain mainly text (words). Microsoft Word is one of the most widely-used word processors.

Getting Started

▶ Turn on your computer and log on in the usual way. You will see the Windows 2000 desktop.

The Office shortcut toolbar

The Word icon

The Start menu

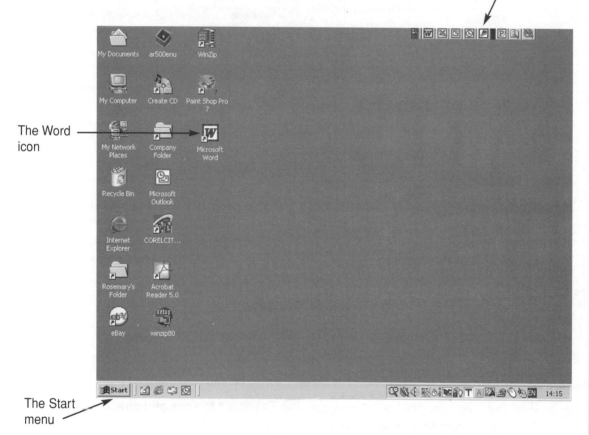

Figure 4.1: The Windows 2000 Desktop

Starting Microsoft Word

Load Microsoft Word in one of the following ways:

1. By clicking on the **Word** icon on the Office Shortcut toolbar.

2. By clicking on the **Word** icon on the desktop. ————————

3. By clicking on the **Start** menu and selecting **Programs, Microsoft Word**.

Chapter 4
Word Processing

1

You will then see the Word opening screen with a document called **Document1** ready for you to start to type.

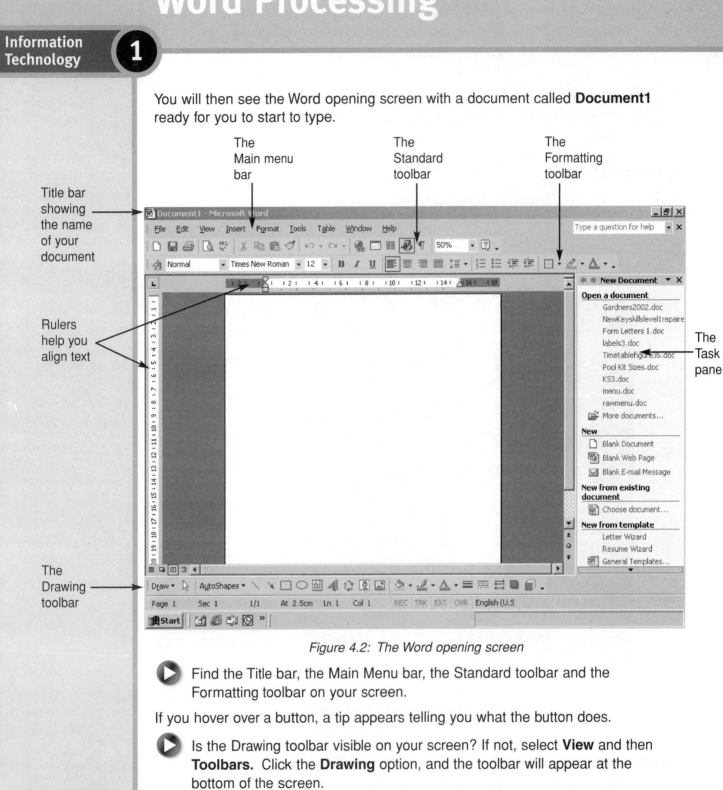

The Main menu bar

The Standard toolbar

The Formatting toolbar

Title bar showing the name of your document

Rulers help you align text

The Task pane

The Drawing toolbar

Figure 4.2: The Word opening screen

▶ Find the Title bar, the Main Menu bar, the Standard toolbar and the Formatting toolbar on your screen.

If you hover over a button, a tip appears telling you what the button does.

▶ Is the Drawing toolbar visible on your screen? If not, select **View** and then **Toolbars**. Click the **Drawing** option, and the toolbar will appear at the bottom of the screen.

▶ The Task pane on the right of the screen can be used to create a new document or open a previously created document. You don't need this at the moment so click the **Close** icon in the top right of the Task pane.

Work through the instructions below to create an advertisement for a part-time job at Broomhill

Creating and saving a document

 Type the advertisement exactly as shown in Figure 4.3, including all the spelling mistakes. Ignore any underlining in red that may appear in the text. Remember to press the **Enter** key only when you want to start a new paragraph.

> Broomhill Sports Club
> Requires a
> Part-time Sports Assistant
>
> Broomhill is a hugly successful Sports Club with a welth of activities on offer. The successful applicant must be prepared to assist with any of these activities as required, together with some administrative tasks. Good communication skills, both written and verbal, are also esential.
>
> This is an exciting opportunity for a lively, dynamic individual, interested in all aspects of fitness and who is happy to work outside normal office hours.
>
> This post would suit a young person studying on a sports/leisure course at college. Training on all items of equipment will bee provided.
> Please apply in writing, enclosing a current CV to:
>
> Mr P Grey
> Manager
> Broomhill Sports Club
> Hale Road
> East Harling
> Essex
> CR8 9JK

Figure 4.3: The text of the advertisement

 Select **File**, **Save** or click the **Save** button on the Standard toolbar. ———

Figure 4.4: The Save As menu

▶ Use the **Save in** drop-down box to find where to save your work. Ask your teacher if you are not sure.

▶ Click in the **File name** box and type the file name **Jobadvert**.

▶ Press **Enter** or click the **Save** button.

Selecting text and changing style

You need to select text in order to change what you have typed. There are several ways of doing this.

❗ You can click and drag the mouse to select the text you want. This is the most usual but not always the most efficient.

❗ Double-click a word to select it or triple-click to select a paragraph.

❗ Click once in the left margin to select the current line, twice to select the current paragraph, and three times to select the entire document.

▶ Practise selecting parts of the advert using these different techniques.

▶ Select the job title (e.g. **Part-time Sports Assistant**).

▶ Make the text bold and underlined by clicking the **Bold** button and the **Underline** button on the Formatting toolbar.

▶ Click in the right-hand margin to deselect the text.

To select click in the left-hand margin

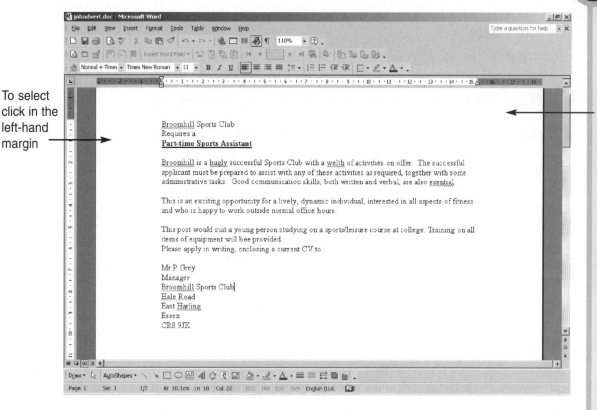

To deselect click in the right-hand margin

Figure 4.5: Selecting text

Aligning text

The company name and job title should be centered on the page.

 Select the first three lines and click the **Center** button on the Formatting toolbar.

Note that there is also an **Align Left** button and an **Align Right** button on the Formatting toolbar – try these out too.

The **Justify** button aligns text with both the left and right margins by spreading the words evenly between the margins (columns in newspapers are often aligned this way).

Cut and Paste

Suppose you want to change the order of the first and second paragraphs. Instead of deleting text and retyping you can use the Cut and Paste feature.

▶ Select the first paragraph by double-clicking in the left margin.

▶ Select **Edit, Cut** or click the **Cut** button from the Standard toolbar.

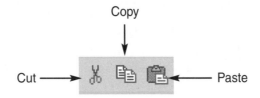

Figure 4.6: The Cut, Copy and Paste buttons

▶ Click the mouse at the end of the second paragraph.

▶ Press the **Enter** key twice.

▶ Select **Edit, Paste** or click the **Paste** button from the Standard toolbar.

 ▶ Click the **Save** button from the Standard toolbar to save your changes.

Check you have only one blank line left after the heading and in between the paragraphs of text. You can delete a blank line by clicking at the beginning of the line and pressing the **Backspace** key on the keyboard.

The **Copy** button works in a similar way to the **Cut** button but copies the text into the Clipboard instead of deleting it. When the text is pasted, the original text is still on the page.

Drag and Drop is another way of moving text. To use this method select the text you wish to move and then move the mouse pointer over the selected text until it changes to a left-pointing arrow. You can then click and drag the text to its new position.

Checking spelling and grammar

You will have noticed several spelling mistakes in the advertisement you have typed.

▶ Click at the beginning of the text.

▶ Select **Tools**, **Spelling and Grammar** or click the **Spelling and Grammar** button on the Standard toolbar.

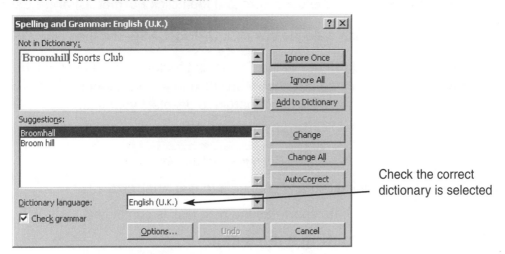

Figure 4.7: The Spelling and Grammar menu

Check the correct dictionary is selected

Word will underline what it considers to be the first error in the top pane – a spelling error will be underlined in red. Suggested corrections are shown in the lower pane.

❗ The first word underlined is **Broomhill**. Although this word cannot be found in the dictionary it is correct, so click the **Ignore All** button.

❗ The next word underlined is **hugly.** The correct spelling is already highlighted in the lower pane, so click the **Change** button.

❗ Correct **welth** and **esential** by using the **Change** button in the same way.

❗ The last word to be highlighted by the spell-checker is **Harling**. This word cannot be found in the dictionary but it is correct so click the **Ignore All** button.

Word underlines most **names** such as **Harling**, so be careful not to correct words that are spelt correctly.

Look at the last paragraph and you will probably spot a deliberate mistake!
In the Spelling and Grammar check earlier, Word did not prompt you to change the word **bee** even though it should read **be**. This is because it is a word and it is spelt correctly. Select the word **bee**, press the **Delete** key, and replace it with the word **be**.

▶ Select **File**, **Save** or click the **Save** button to save your changes.

Always **proof-read** a document when you have finished. Do **not** rely on Word to correct every mistake for you!

Tip:

If you want to find all occurrences of a certain word and replace it with a different word, try using Find and Replace:

Select **Edit**, **Replace** and enter the change you want to make.

Formatting text

Word provides you with different fonts (type styles), sizes, colours and alignments that you can select for all or part of your document.

You have already used the Bold and Underline styles. Now try changing some text to a different font and size.

▶ Select the first line of the document and then click **Format**, **Change Case**.

▶ In the Change Case dialogue box click **UPPERCASE** and then click **OK.**

▶ Click in the drop-down box in the Formatting toolbar and select the font **Bauhaus 93** and in the drop-down box next to it, select font size **20**. Click anywhere in the right-hand margin to deselect your text.

Figure 4.8: Changing font and font size

▶ Select the remaining text and change it to font Arial, size 12.

Other formatting features are shown as the next task is completed.

Print Preview and Printing a document

Follow the steps below to print the advertisement.

 ▶ Click the **Print Preview** button on the Standard toolbar

BROOMHILL SPORTS CLUB
Requires a
Part-time Sports Assistant

This is an exciting opportunity for a lively, dynamic individual, interested in all aspects of fitness and who is happy to work outside normal office hours.

Broomhill is a hugely successful Sports Club with a wealth of activities on offer. The successful applicant must be prepared to assist with any of these activities as required, together with some administrative tasks. Good communication skills, both written and verbal, are also essential.

This post would suit a young person studying on a sports/leisure course at college. Training on all items of equipment will be provided.
Please apply in writing, enclosing a current CV to:

Mr P Grey
Manager
Broomhill Sports Club
Hale Road
East Harling
Essex
CR8 9JK

Figure 4.9

▶ Check the preview on the screen carefully to make sure that it is exactly what you want. If it is not correct any errors.

 ▶ Click the **Print** button on the toolbar and collect your printout.

▶ Save your advertisement and close the document by selecting **File**, **Close**.

Tip:

Always Print Preview your document before you print it out, it will save a lot of trees!

Produce the menu for a dinner at the Broomhill Sports Club Restaurant

 Open Word if it is not already open.

 Click the **New Blank Document** button. —————————————

 Type the text exactly as shown in Figure 4.10, ignoring the boxes on the left.

Bauhaus 93 size 26	Broomhill Sports Club
Lucida Calligraphy size 16 bold	Valentine's Day Dinner
Arial size 12	14th February 2002
Lucida Calligraphy size 14 bold Arial size 12	Starters Clear vegetable soup with crispy croutons Smoked salmon with a mustard sauce Spicy scallops in white wine
Lucida Calligraphy size 14 bold Arial size 12	Main Courses Poached salmon steak with tarragon Beef Wellington Mushroom risotto Chicken breast stuffed with stilton and herbs
Lucida Calligraphy size 14 bold Arial size 12	Desserts Strawberry gateau Lemon and lime cheesecake Chocolate indulgence pie
Arial size 12	Coffee and mints
Arial size 14 bold	We hope you enjoy your evening

Figure 4.10: The text for the menu

 Save the document with the name **Menu**.

 Try to format the text using the fonts and sizes shown to the left of Figure 4.10.

 Centre the menu by selecting the text and clicking the **Center** button on the Formatting toolbar.

Chapter 4
Word Processing

Inserting a border

Insert a decorative border around the menu as follows:

▶ Select all the text.

▶ Select **Format**, **Borders and Shading** and click on the **Borders** tab.

▶ Choose the **Box** setting, **Apply to Paragraph** and a style of your choice.

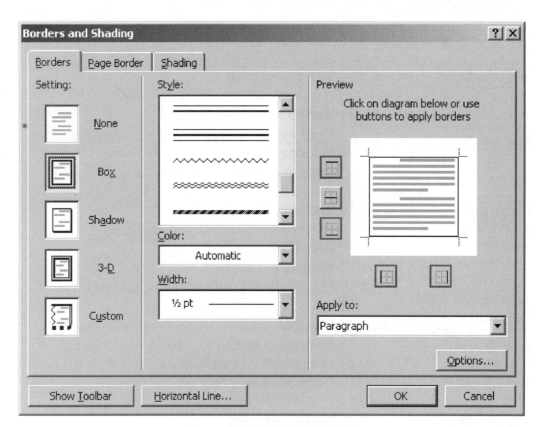

Figure 4.11: Creating a border

Inserting clip art

This is a special dinner so the menu could look more interesting! Microsoft Word is supplied with a selection of pictures called clip art which you can use, or you might have other CDs with clip art images. If not, there is a plentiful supply available (copyright-free) from the Microsoft web site.

To smarten up the menu, search the local clip art gallery to find an appropriate picture and some dividers to separate the courses (see Figure 4.13).

▶ Click underneath the first line and select **Insert**, **Picture**, **Clip Art**.

Figure 4.12: Searching for clip art

▶ The Task pane will reappear on the right. In the Search text box enter the word **valentines** and click on **Search**.

▶ Scroll through the images, find a suitable one and double-click it.

▶ It will automatically be inserted into your document. Drag it to the correct position and size it using the black squares around it (known as 'handles'). Drag one of the corner handles to keep the width and height of the image to the same scale.

▶ If your clip art will not move, click it and select **Format**, **Picture**. Click the **Layout** tab and choose **In front of text**. Click **OK**. The handles should now be white and you can move the picture.

▶ Click **Modify** in the Task pane and then search the clip art gallery using the word **dividers** and find a fancy line to separate the courses. Size the lines to fit.

▶ Save your work.

Your menu should now be looking something like this:

Broomhill Sports Club

Valentine's Day Dinner

14th February 2002

Starters
Clear vegetable soup with crispy croutons
Smoked salmon with a mustard sauce
Spicy scallops in white wine

Main Courses
Poached salmon steak with tarragon
Beef Wellington
Mushroom risotto
Chicken breast stuffed with stilton and herbs

Desserts
Strawberry gateau
Lemon and lime cheesecake
Chocolate indulgence pie

Coffee and mints

We hope you enjoy your evening

Figure 4.13: The completed menu

Produce a list of sports equipment

Using bullets

The Sports Club needs a list of all the equipment they hire out to customers.

▶ Open a new document and type the heading **Sports Equipment for Hire.**

▶ Press **Enter** twice to leave a blank line.

▶ Click the **Bullets** button on the Formatting toolbar. ——————————

▶ Look at the extract from the Broomhill brochure shown on page 9.
Type in the items of equipment the club are likely to hire out.
After each item press **Enter.**

Sports Equipment for Hire

- Tennis racquets
- Table tennis bats
- Badminton racquets
- Squash racquets
- Etc. etc.

Figure 4.14

> **Tip:**
> A 'bullet' is a dot or some other symbol inserted before items in a list for emphasis.

Numbered lists

Items in a list can be automatically numbered. Instead of clicking the **Bullets** button on the Formatting toolbar, click the **Numbering** button. ———————

▶ Convert your list of equipment into a numbered list by selecting the list and clicking the **Numbering** button.

Sample task | **Create a staff rota**

Using tabs

One way of producing lists arranged in columns is to set **Tab Stops** and use the **Tab** key to move between these set positions.

Microsoft Word has default tab positions which appear as faint marks below the ruler underneath the Formatting toolbar.

Default tab stops

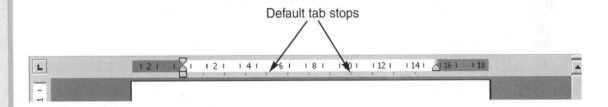

Figure 4.15

The default tab stops in the screenshot above are 1.27cm apart.

 Open a new document and try out the tabs by typing the list below. Don't use the Spacebar at all. Use the **Tab** key (to the left of the letter **Q** on the keyboard) to move between columns. Sometimes you may have to press the **Tab** key more than once.

STAFF ROTA (weekdays)

Monday	**Tuesday**	**Wednesday**	**Thursday**	**Friday**
Julie	Dave	Sherif	Anna	Caroline
Steffi	Pierre	Carla	Boris	Brian
Hans	Susan	Bonita	Marga	Paul

Figure 4.16

Another way of arranging information in neat columns is to insert a table into your document. You will have a go at that next.

Create a table showing the membership fees for Broomhill Sports Club

Using tables

The Manager wants a neat list of membership fees to pin up on the club's notice board.

▶ Open a new document by clicking the **New Blank Document** button from the Standard toolbar.

▶ Type the heading **Annual Membership Fees - Unlimited Use,** select the text and format it as **Arial** size **14, Bold** and **Centred.** Press **Enter** twice.

▶ Change the font to **Arial,** size **12,** not bold, left-aligned.

▶ Select **Table, Insert, Table** and select **4** columns and **5** rows. Click **OK.**

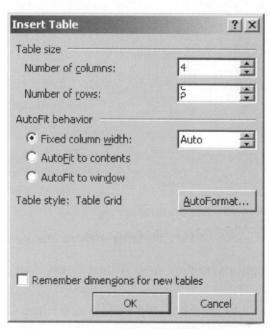

Figure 4.17: The Insert Table dialogue box

A blank table is created as shown below

a column

a row ⟶

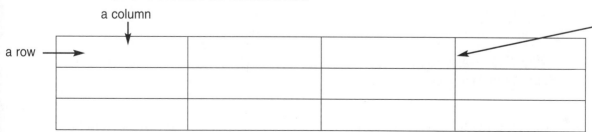

Figure 4.18: The blank table

> **Tip:**
> You can also use the **Insert Table** button from the Standard toolbar.
>
>

> **Tip:**
> Drag the line between two columns to adjust column width. The cursor changes to a double-headed arrow.
>
>

▶ Type the text shown in Figure 4.20. (You will format the text in a minute.)

▶ Select columns 2, 3 and 4 by dragging over them and **Centre** the text.

▶ Size the columns to make the table look like Figure 4.20 by dragging the line between two columns.

▶ Select the column headings by clicking once in the left margin, next to the headings. Click the **Bold** button.

▶ Select the row headings by dragging and click the **Bold** button.

▶ Select the column headings again. Select **Format, Borders and Shading** and choose the **Shading** tab. Select **Gray 10%** and click **OK**.

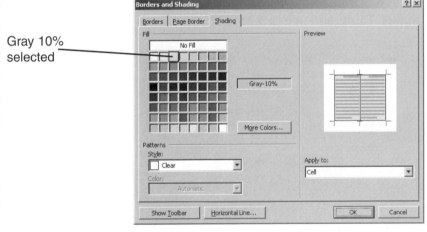

Figure 4.19: The Shading tab with Gray 10% selected

▶ Select the first column and shade **Gray 10%** in the same way.

▶ Save the document using the name **AnnualFees**. Your document should look like Figure 4.20.

Annual Membership Fees - Unlimited Use

	For one person	Joint membership	Family membership
Full Membership	£250	£350	£400
Swimming only	£100	£150	£200
Gym only	£125	£175	N/A
Sauna/Sunbed	£75	£125	£150

Figure 4.20: The completed table

▶ Click the **Print Preview** button, check carefully then click the **Print** button and save your work.

> **Tip:**
> You can also select a column by moving the mouse pointer over the column header until it becomes a down-arrow, and then clicking the left mouse button.

Produce an A4 poster for the club gym

You have been asked to produce an eye-catching poster to advertise the club gym. This type of document, together with others like newsletters, invitations, advertisements and even newspapers are often produced using software called **Desktop Publishing** (DTP). Microsoft Publisher is an example of this type of software. However, the latest versions of Microsoft Word have a lot of DTP features too. We will try out some of them here.

Changing the page layout

▶ Open a new document by clicking the **New Blank Document** button on the Standard toolbar.

▶ Select **File**, **Page Setup**.

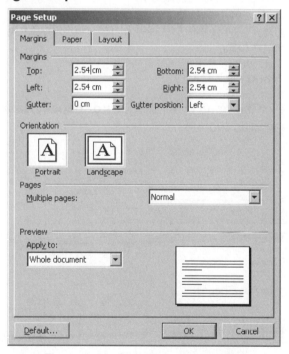

Figure 4.21: Changing page settings

▶ Click on **Landscape** and click **OK**.

Portrait   Landscape

> **Tip:**
> You can also use this box to change the size of the **margins** – the white border at the top, bottom, left and right of a page.

> **Tip:**
> A document in **Portrait** orientation is taller than it is wide, like this page. **Landscape** orientation is used for short, wide pages.

▶ Type in the heading **Broomhill Sports Club** in **Bauhaus 93** font, size **48**, **bold** and **centred.**

▶ Press **Enter** and type **Gym Facilities.** Use the **Font Color** tool on the Formatting toolbar to make this text blue, and press **Enter.**

Using drawing tools

We will now create a graphic to denote the gym.

▶ Make sure the Drawing toolbar is displayed. If it isn't, click **View, Toolbars** and select it.

▶ Use the **Rectangle** tool to draw the body.

▶ Make the body black using the **Fill** tool.

▶ Draw one arm using the **Rectangle** tool.

▶ Shade the arm by clicking the **Fill** tool arrow, selecting **Fill Effects** and clicking the **Pattern** tab.

▶ Select a pattern and click **OK**.

▶ Draw a triangle for the hand by clicking **AutoShapes**, **Basic Shapes** and selecting the isosceles triangle.

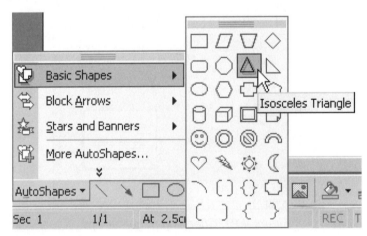

▶ Shade the hand with the same pattern as the arm.

▶ Use the **Rectangle** tool and the **Oval** tool to create one of the weights just overlapping the hand. Fill the weight with black.

▶ Bring the hand in front of the weight by right-clicking the hand and selecting **Order, Bring to Front,** from the shortcut menu.

▶ Use the **Select Objects** tool to drag around the arm, hand and weight.

▶ Right-click and select **Grouping, Group.**

▶ The arm, hand and weight are now grouped as one object. Select **Edit, Copy** and then **Edit, Paste** to copy the arm, hand and weight.

▶ That's fine, but it's pointing the wrong way! Select **Draw, Rotate or Flip, Flip Horizontal.**

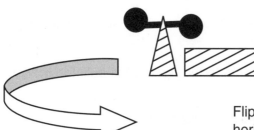

Flip the copy of the arm horizontally to create the left arm.

▶ Drag the left arm into position.

▶ Finally use the **Oval** tool to draw the head and fill it with the same pattern as the arms.

▶ Double-click beneath the graphic and click the **Align Left** button on the Formatting toolbar.

▶ Enter the bulleted list of activities:

- Treadmills
- Rowing machines
- Ski walkers
- Stairclimbers
- Weights
- Exercise bikes
- Cross-trainers
- Personal fitness programmes

▶ Highlight the list and keep clicking the **Increase Indent** button on the Formatting toolbar until the list is positioned in the centre of the page.

▶ Draw a text box for the opening times using the **Text Box** tool.

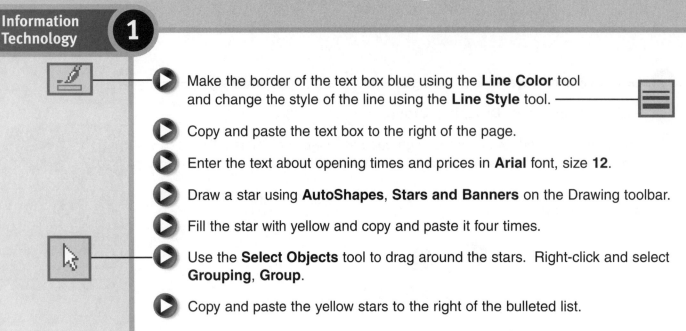

▶ Make the border of the text box blue using the **Line Color** tool and change the style of the line using the **Line Style** tool.

▶ Copy and paste the text box to the right of the page.

▶ Enter the text about opening times and prices in **Arial** font, size **12**.

▶ Draw a star using **AutoShapes**, **Stars and Banners** on the Drawing toolbar.

▶ Fill the star with yellow and copy and paste it four times.

▶ Use the **Select Objects** tool to drag around the stars. Right-click and select **Grouping**, **Group**.

▶ Copy and paste the yellow stars to the right of the bulleted list.

Your poster should be looking something like this:

Figure 4.22

Exercise 1: Create a poster to advertise one of the other sports facilities at the club. Use a selection of the word processing features you have learned in this chapter.

Sample Assignment

Background

You work for a travel operator who produces a catalogue for summer holidays each year. Unfortunately details of a new hotel on the island of Majorca were received after the latest catalogue had gone to print. You are asked to produce an A4 page that can be given to anyone enquiring about this area.

Tasks

1   Pick up a travel brochure from a travel agent, find an appropriate reference CD-ROM or use the Internet to find some information about Majorca.

2   Read the information you have found and print out what might be useful for your document. Select the most relevant parts using a highlighter pen and annotate by hand.

3   Use MS Word to create the A4 page. The page you produce should include:

   • A table of maximum monthly temperatures.

   • A suitable picture of the island that you need to crop and resize.
     You could ask your teacher to help you scan a picture or you could use a picture off the Internet.

   • Different sizes, styles and colours of text.

   • An example of the use of one or more drawing tools.

   • Some clip art.

4   Experiment with different formatting and layout to achieve the most professional-looking result.

5   Keep all your draft printouts and make hand-written notes on them to explain what was wrong.

6   Spell-check and proof-read the document carefully.

7   Save the file with an appropriate name.

8   Make a backup of the file.

9   Use the **Print Screen** key to show where and how the files are stored.

Evidence to collect

• Notes of where you found information.

• The information you printed out with the most important parts highlighted.

• A copy of the original picture before it was cropped and sized.

• Annotated draft printouts of the document.

• The final document.

• Screenshot of Windows Explorer to show the file and backup file saved on disk.

Chapter 4
Word Processing

Relating the assignment to the specification

Specification Reference (Part B)	What has been done to satisfy this
IT1.1	
• Find and select relevant information.	• Tasks 1 and 2
• Enter and bring in information, using formats that help development.	• Tasks 3 and 4
• Explore and develop information to meet your purpose.	• Tasks 4, 5 and 6
IT1.2	
• Use appropriate layouts for presenting information in a consistent way.	• Tasks 3 and 4
• Develop the presentation so that it is accurate, clear and meets your purpose.	• Tasks 4, 5, and 6
• Save information so that it can be found easily.	• Tasks 7, 8, and 9

Other Key Skills signposting

Communication C1.3

Ideas for other assignments

 A word-processed assignment for your main area of study (including a table of numbers).

A letter applying for a job, together with a C.V.

A price list for a hairdressing salon.

A research report including a table (see Communications assignment 3).

A restaurant menu.

An advertising flyer for a new nightclub.

Sample test questions

1   You create an invitation to a New Year's Eve party using a graphics software package. You may need to change it and use it again in future years. To keep it for this purpose it must be:

    A   created in a spreadsheet package

    B   very colourful

    C   saved

    D   printed

2   In a long word-processed document the name 'Mr Black' has been incorrectly referred to as 'Mr Brown'. What feature could best be used to correct the error?

    A   spell check

    B   find and replace

    C   change case

    D   format

Here is an extract from a magazine.

> Perhaps your grill is unreliable or the thermostat has gone on your oven - or maybe you are planning a complete overhaul of your kitchen. Either way it is probably time to be looking for a new cooker. There are currently some excellent deals on offer. For example:
>
> Servis TE600, free-standing, £529; Stoves 700FDOA, free-standing, £2,000; ATAG OX611T, built-in, £1,225; Brandt FLC 24, built-in, £750; Bosch HBN 7050, built-in, £870.
>
> These are just a few, the choice is huge, but the type of fuel you use and the space available in your kitchen will influence your choice.

Figure 1

Questions 3 to 5 are based on Figure 1

3   To check the spelling of the extract in Figure 1, it is essential that the correct:

    A   spreadsheet package is used

    B   language is selected

    C   date is entered

    D   web browser is used

4   The text in Figure 1 is:

    A   centered

    B   right-justified

    C   left-justified

    D   justified

5   The information in the second paragraph of the extract in Figure 1 would be clearer:

    A   displayed as a table

    B   without prices

    C   in capital letters

    D   if the prices were written in words

A hairdresser has designed the following leaflet to send to its customers.

Figure 2

Questions 6 to 14 are based on figure 2

6   Which one of the following software packages might be used to produce this leaflet?

    A   word processing

    B   web browser

    C   virus checker

    D   spreadsheet

7   What has been used to make the list clearer?

    A   simple words

    B   icons

    C   numbers

    D   bullets

8   When producing a leaflet like this, the text box can often get lost behind the graphic images. This can be rectified by using the facility called:

    A   group

    B   order

    C   merge

    D   delete

9   What additional information would be useful to customers on this leaflet?

    A   opening times

    B   stylist's name

    C   filename

    D   file size

10   A long price list is to be added to the leaflet. It would be best to present this form of information in:

    A   pictures

    B   words

    C   a table

    D   a numbered list

11   The pictures used on this leaflet are likely to have been inserted from:

    A   a digital camera

    B   clip art

    C   an oil painting

    D   a photograph

12   The graphic images of the scissors can be removed from the leaflet by selecting and:

    A   sizing

    B   copying

    C   cropping

    D   deleting

13   The best way for a garage to advertise electronically would be to use:

    A   a word-processed printed leaflet

    B   e-mails

    C   a web site

    D   posters

14   A spare parts company publishes its very large catalogue in a format suitable for use on a computer. The most likely format would be:

    A   DVD

    B   floppy disk

    C   capital letters

    D   CD-ROM

Chapter 5
Spreadsheets

Spreadsheets are used mainly for working with numbers. They are used in many different applications which involve calculations or drawing charts. Microsoft Excel is one of many different spreadsheet packages. In Excel, spreadsheets are referred to as workbooks. Just to make it even more confusing, a workbook can contain several worksheets.

The Excel opening screen

▶ Log on to your computer in the usual way.

▶ Start Excel in one of the following ways, depending how your system has been set up:

* By clicking on the **Excel** icon on the Office shortcut bar.
* By clicking on the **Excel** icon on the desktop.
* By clicking **Start**, **Programs**, **Microsoft Excel**.

You will then see the Excel opening screen, with a blank worksheet ready for you to start work.

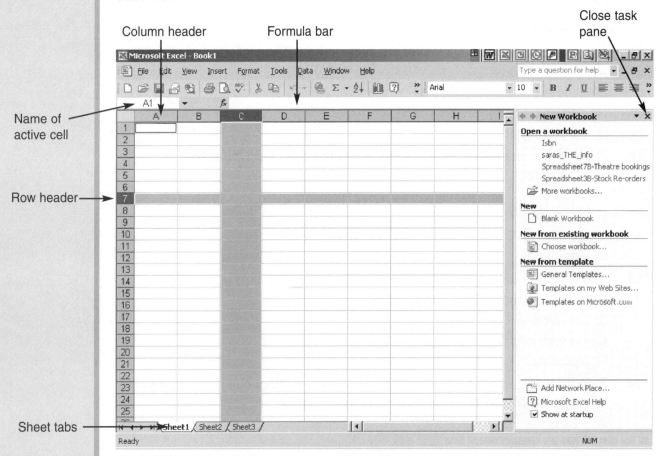

Figure 5.1: The Excel Opening screen

If you are using Office XP you will see the Task pane on the right of your screen.

▶ Close the Task pane by clicking the **X** in the top right-hand corner.

Moving round the worksheet

You can tell where you are on the screen by looking in the Name box or by seeing which cell has the heavy border round it. This is known as the **active cell.** Anything you type appears in both the **active cell** and the **formula bar.** Your sheet is much larger than the area shown on the screen so get used to moving around in the following ways:

▶ Use the mouse to click in the cell you want.

▶ Use the scroll bars to move to a different area of the sheet and then click on the cell you want.

▶ Use the **Page Up** and **Page Down** keys**.**

▶ Select **Edit/Go To** and type a cell reference.

▶ Press **Ctrl-Home** to return to cell A1.

▶ Press **Ctrl-End** to move to the last cell in your sheet.

Chapter 5
Spreadsheets

Information
Technology **1**

Sample task

Prepare a spreadsheet that displays the usage figures for different facilities at the Sports Club

Entering data

Follow the instructions given below. The data will look like this:

Tip:
You will notice that data starting with a letter is automatically left-justified in a cell. Numeric data on the other hand is automatically right-justified.

Microsoft Excel - Book1

File Edit View Insert Format Tools Data Window Help test

100% B

G12 *fx*

	A	B	C	D	E	F	G
1	Facility	No. of hours used		Average			
2		Yr 2000	Yr 2001				
3	Swimming pool	4545	4699				
4	Gym	4306	4589				
5	Badminton courts	6156	6044				
6	Aerobics suite	1080	1440				
7	Squash courts	6548	6455				
8	Tennis courts	4928	4822				
9							
10	Total						
11							

Figure 5.2: Entering the data

▶ Click in cell A1. Type the heading **Facility.**

▶ Press the right arrow key. Type the heading **No. of hours used.**

▶ Press the right arrow key twice and type **Average** in cell D1.

 ▶ Highlight cells B1 and C1 and click the **Merge Cells** button on the Formatting toolbar. This will merge the two cells together.

▶ Copy the other information from Figure 5.2 into your spreadsheet.

▶ Make column A wider so that you can see all of the text by clicking between column A and column B and dragging to the right. Alternatively you can double-click between column A and column B to automatically size the column.

▶ Click in cell D1 and then click the **Align Right** button on the Formatting toolbar to move the heading to the right of the cell.

▶ Right-align cells B2 and C2 and make them bold by clicking the **Bold** button on the Formatting toolbar.

▶ Highlight cells A1 to D1 and make them bold.

▶ Make cells A3 to A10 bold in the same way.

58

Inserting and deleting rows and columns

We can delete the whole of row 9 so that no gap is left between the list and the label **Total.**

▶ Right-click the row header for row 9. Select **Delete** from the shortcut menu.

▶ Click the left mouse button.

The label **Total** moves up to row 9.

Now, suppose we want to put a heading at the top of the worksheet. We need to insert a row.

▶ Right-click the row header for row 1.

▶ Select **Insert** from the shortcut menu.

▶ Click the left mouse button.

▶ Type **Broomhill Sports Club** in cell A1 of the new row and press **Enter.**

▶ Make the title **bold** and **14** pt.

▶ Insert another blank line yourself beneath this new title.

Saving your work

It is important to save your work regularly into an area of the computer that you will be able to find again, and to use a filename that you will remember!

Your teacher may need to show you which folder to save your file in.

▶ Click **File** on the main menu, then **Save.**

Excel automatically gives your workbook the default name **Book1.xls.** The name will be highlighted so that it is selected ready for you to change it.

▶ Type a new name **Facilities** and click **Save.**

Chapter 5
Spreadsheets

Entering formulae

The main use of a spreadsheet is to calculate results using formulae. The following mathematical symbols are used:

+	Add
-	Subtract
*	Multiply
/	Divide
()	Brackets

We will calculate the total number of hours the facilities were used for in the year 2000. Formulae are entered using cell references.

▶ Click in cell B11.

▶ Type an equals sign (=) to tell Excel that you are about to enter a formula.

▶ Type **B5+B6+B7+B8+B9+B10** so that the formula appears as shown in Figure 5.3.

Note: If you are using Office XP you will see different coloured lines appear around the cells – just ignore them!

	A	B	C	D	E
1	**Broomhill Sports Club**				
2					
3	Facility	No. of hours used		Average	
4		Yr 2000	Yr 2001		
5	Swimming pool	4545	4699		
6	Gym	4306	4589		
7	Badminton courts	6156	6044		
8	Aerobics suite	1080	1440		
9	Squash courts	6548	6455		
10	Tennis courts	4928	4822		
11	Total	=B5+B6+B7+B8+B9+B10			
12					
13					

Figure 5.3

▶ Press **Enter.** The answer appears!

Exercise 1: In cell C11, calculate the total number of hours used in 2001.

Using Autosum

A much quicker way of adding up a list (or row) of numbers is to use the **Autosum** button. ────────────────────────

Σ

▶ Highlight cells B11 and C11 and press the **Delete** key to clear the cells.

▶ Click in cell B11 and click the **Autosum** button.

Excel guesses which cells you want to sum. Your screen will look like the one below.

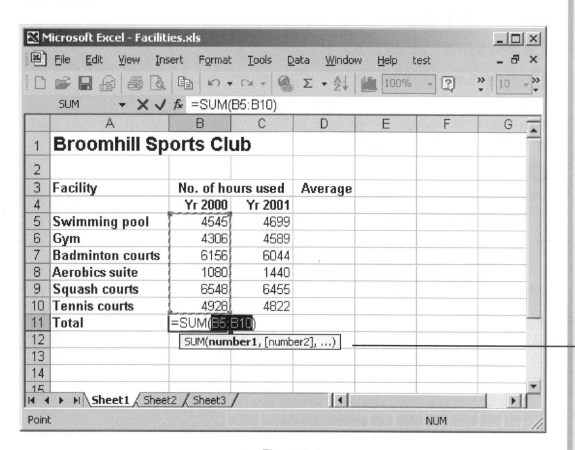

Tip:
In Office XP you will see a tip in a yellow box beneath the formula. Don't worry about it - it's just for information.

Figure 5.4

▶ Press **Enter**. The answer appears.

Exercise 2: Use **Autosum** to calculate the Total in cell C11 in the same way.

Using Functions

Excel has over 200 built-in functions to perform different mathematical calculations for you. You have already used one without realising it. If you look at the formula bar in Figure 5.4 you will see that the **Autosum** button automatically entered the SUM function for you. You can also enter a function by typing it into the cell. We will try this by calculating the average number of hours each facility was used over the two years.

▶ Click in cell D5.

▶ Type =**average(** in the cell.

▶ Select cells B5 and C5. Type **)** to finish the formula.

▶ Press **Enter.** The answer 4622 appears in the cell.

To calculate the averages for the other facilities you can just copy the formula down the column using the **AutoFill** feature.

▶ Click in cell D5.

▶ Click and drag the little square in the bottom right-hand corner of the cell. This is called the **fill handle.** Drag it to cell D10.

The other averages will automatically be calculated for you.

Note: In Office XP an **AutoFill options** button will appear – ignore this at present.

Formatting Numbers

The average number of hours needs to be shown in integer format (whole numbers with no decimal places). We need to format the numbers in column D.

▶ Select cells D5 to D10 by dragging across them. You could also select the whole of column D by clicking in the column header.

▶ Click the **Decrease Decimal** button on the Formatting toolbar. ——————

We will now add a column showing the average revenue generated by the different facilities.

▶ Enter a heading **Revenue** into cell E3.

▶ Enter the following figures into cells E5 to E10.

> 110306
> 111200
> 12200
> 63000
> 22757
> 24375

▶ In cell E11 calculate the total revenue from these facilities using the **AutoSum** button.

▶ Highlight cells E5 to E11 and click the **Currency** button on the Formatting ——————
toolbar. This will format the numbers as currency.

▶ Right-align the heading **Revenue** and make it **bold.**

Adding borders and shading

▶ Press the **Print Preview** button on the Standard toolbar.

The table will be easier to read if it has borders around each cell so that you can see which column and row you are in.

▶ Press the **Esc** key to leave Print Preview mode.

▶ Select cells A3 to E11.

▶ Click the down arrow next to the **Borders** button on the Formatting toolbar.

▶ Select the border option shown in Figure 5.5.

> **Tip:**
> Try out the Increase Decimal button too – it looks the same but the arrow points the other way.

Chapter 5
Spreadsheets

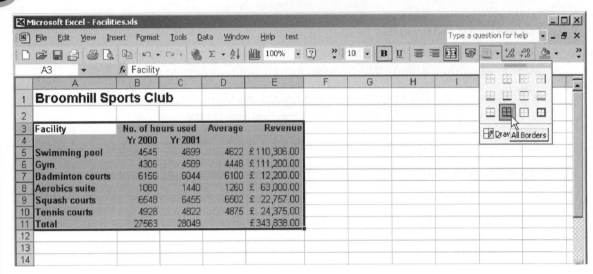

Figure 5.5: Selecting a border

▶ Highlight cells A1 to C1.

▶ Select the **Border** drop-down box from the Formatting toolbar and select the **Thick Box** border.

▶ Select the **Fill Colour** drop-down box from the Formatting toolbar and select **Gray-25%**.

The spreadsheet should look something like this:

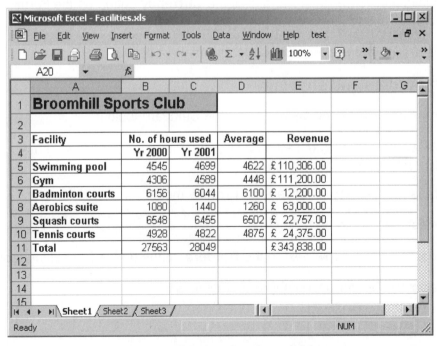

Figure 5.6: The completed spreadsheet

Printing the spreadsheet

Remember always to check exactly what your sheet will look like before printing.

▶ Click the **Save** button on the Standard toolbar.

▶ Click the **Print Preview** button on the Standard toolbar. ─────────────

A preview of the page appears. You can click on the **Zoom** button to get a larger view of the page.

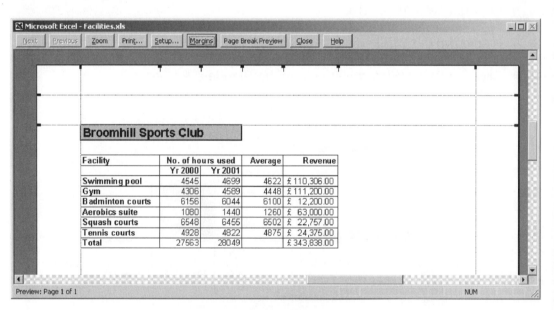

Figure 5.7: Print Preview mode

▶ When you are sure that your sheet is exactly how you want it, click the **Print** button from within Print Preview mode.

▶ The Print dialogue box appears. Click **OK**.

Tip:

To print the spreadsheet showing the formulae: Select **Tools**, **Options** and click the **View** tab. Select the **Formulas** window option and click **OK**.

Prepare a chart that shows how much each individual facility contributes to the total revenue

It is often easier to understand information when it is shown as a chart. A pie chart is used to show the amount each value in a list contributes to the whole. We will draw a pie chart that shows how much each individual facility contributes to the total revenue.

Creating the pie chart

▶ Highlight cells A5 to A10.

▶ Hold down the **Ctrl** key on the keyboard while you select cells E5 to E10.

 ▶ Click the **Chart Wizard** button from the Standard toolbar.

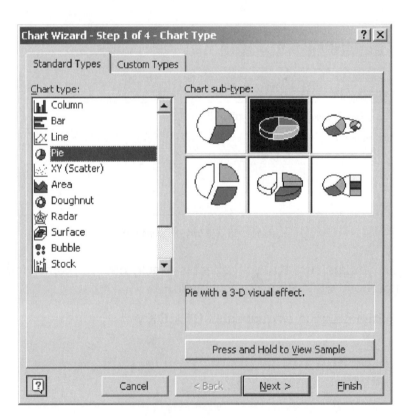

Figure 5.8

▶ Select **Pie** from the Chart types and the **3-D chart** sub-type as shown.

▶ Click the **Next** button to move to step 2 of the wizard.

▶ In Step 2 click the **Next** button to move to Step 3.

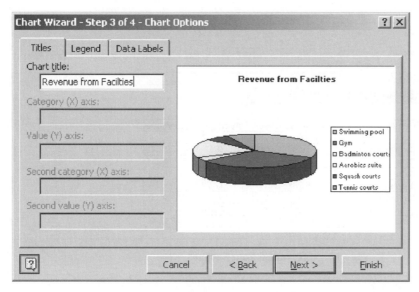

Figure 5.9

▶ Click the **Titles** tab and enter a main heading for the chart as shown above.

▶ Click the **Data Labels** tab and select to display labels as percentages.

▶ Click **Next** to move to Step 4.

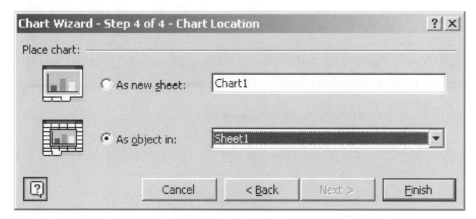

Figure 5.10

▶ In Step 4 leave the option **As object in** selected and click the **Finish** button.

The chart should appear in your sheet. You can drag it and size it as you have done for other objects in earlier chapters.

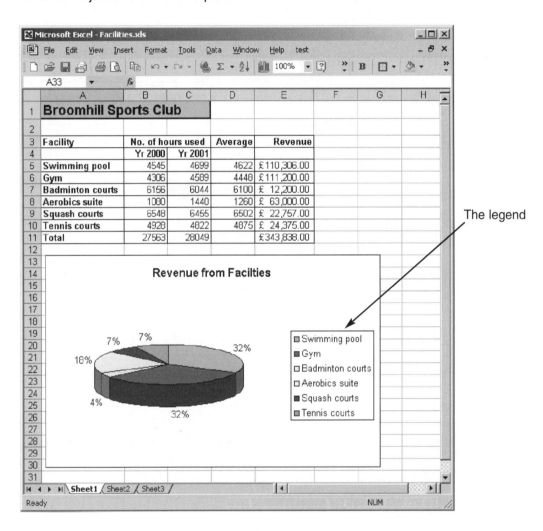

The legend

Figure 5.11

> ## Prepare a chart that shows the number of hours each facility was used in the year 2000 compared to 2001

A bar chart is often used to compare values in different groups or categories. We will create a bar chart to show the number of hours each facility was used in the year 2000 compared to 2001.

Creating the bar chart

▶ Select cells A4 to C10 on your Facilities spreadsheet.

▶ Click the **Chart Wizard** button on the Standard toolbar. ———————

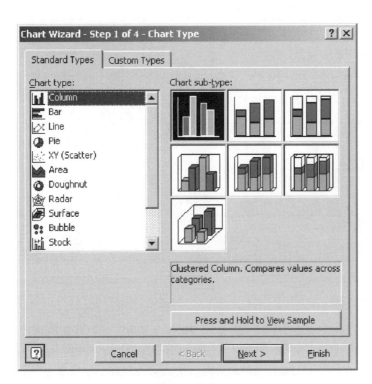

Figure 5.12

Chapter 5
Spreadsheets

▶ Select **Column** from the Chart types and **Clustered column** sub-type as shown above.

▶ Click the **Next** button to move to step 2 of the wizard, then **Next** again.

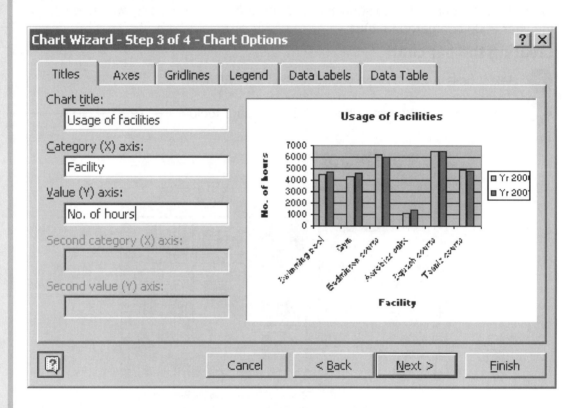

Figure 5.13

▶ In Step 3, click the **Titles** tab and enter a main heading for the chart and titles for the X and Y axes as shown in Figure 5.13.

▶ Click **Next** to move to Step 4.

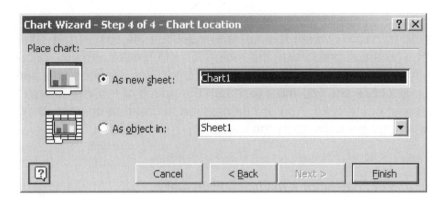

Figure 5.14

▶ In Step 4 select the option **As new sheet** as shown above.

▶ Click **Finish**.

The chart will be created on a new sheet of the workbook. It will be called **Chart1**.

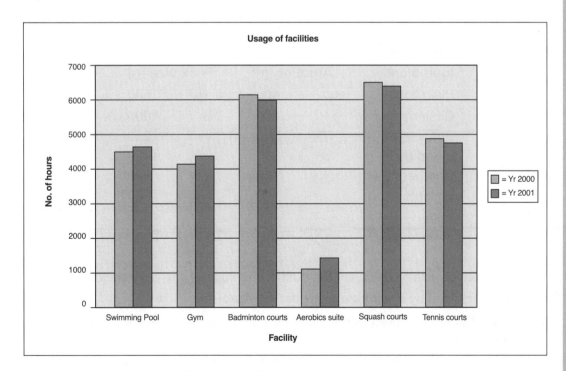

Figure 5.15: The completed bar chart

Exercise 3:   Create a 3-D bar chart to show the revenue generated from the different facilities.

Chapter 5
Spreadsheets

Sample Assignment

Background

You want to bake a cake for your friend's birthday, but you're rather short of cash. You are asked to create two spreadsheets to calculate the cost of two different cakes. First, you are supplied with the recipe for a fruit cake and you calculate the cost of the ingredients and the total cost of the cake. You are then supplied with a recipe for ginger cake and you must research the prices of the ingredients to work out the total cost of the cake. You are then asked to create a chart to show which ingredient in the ginger cake costs the most.

Tasks

1   In Microsoft Excel, enter a main title **Fruit Cake**.

2   Enter the first column heading **Ingredient**, which should be left-aligned.

3   Enter the other column headings (right-aligned) as follows:

Amount (g)   Pack size (g)   Price   Cost

where: **Amount (g)** is the weight of the ingredient required for the cake

Pack size (g) is the weight of a pack of the ingredient.

Price is the price of a pack.

Cost is the cost of the amount of the ingredient required for the cake

4   Enter the data shown below:

Ingredient	Amount (g)	Pack size (g)	Price
Plain flour	400	1500	0.84
Caster sugar	300	1000	0.79
Butter	300	250	0.72
Mixed fruit	850	1000	1.60
Cherries	180	200	0.88
Walnuts	100	200	2.80
Eggs	6	6	0.64
Total Cost			

5   Insert a formula to calculate the cost of the flour for the cake as follows:
Price divided by **Pack size** multiplied by **Amount.**

6   Copy the formula down the column so that the costs of all the ingredients are displayed.

7   In the **Total Cost** row insert a formula at the bottom of the **Cost** column to give the overall cost of the cake.

8   Format the **Price** and **Cost** columns to 2 decimal places.

9   Save and print the spreadsheet.

10   Delete the walnuts to see how much this reduces the cost.

11   Save and print the spreadsheet again.

12   Produce a printout that displays the formulae.

Here is a recipe for ginger cake:

Ginger cake	
Ingredient	**Amount (g)**
Self raising flour	225
Ground ginger	15
Margarine	120
Brown sugar	225
Eggs	1

13   Research the prices of these ingredients. You could visit a supermarket or use an on-line shopping site such as **www.tesco.com**.

14   Set up a spreadsheet for this recipe in the same format as the one for fruit cake.

15   Create a pie chart to show what percentage the cost of each ingredient was of the total cost of the cake.

16   Save and print the spreadsheet and the pie chart.

17   Print the spreadsheet displaying the formulae.

18   Create a backup file of the document.

19   Use the Print Screen function to show saved files.

Compare the spreadsheets for the fruit cake and the ginger cake.

20   Taking into account your shortage of cash, which one will you make for your friend's birthday?

Evidence to collect

*   Any draft printouts marked up to show what was wrong.
*   Three final printouts of the first spreadsheet for tasks 9, 11 and 12.
*   Notes on where you found the information for task 13.
*   Two printouts of the second spreadsheet for tasks 16 and 17.
*   A printout of the pie chart.
*   A printout showing the saved files in Windows Explorer.
*   The answer to task 20 (this can be added to the printout for task 16).

Relating the assignment to the specification

Specification Reference (Part B)	What has been done to satisfy this
IT1.1	
• Find and select relevant information.	• Task 13
• Enter and bring in information, using formats that help development.	• Tasks 3 – 8 and 14 – 15
• Explore and develop information to meet your purpose.	• Tasks 5, 7, 8 and 15
IT1.2	
• Use appropriate layouts for presenting information in a consistent way.	• Tasks 3, 8 and 14
• Develop the presentation so that it is accurate, clear and meets your purpose.	• Task 15
• Save information so that it can be found easily.	• Tasks 16 and 18

Other Key Skills signposting

Number N1.2, N1.3

Communication C1.3

Ideas for other assignments

❗ The results from a Science experiment, including analysis, and including the spreadsheet and/or charts in a word-processed report.

❗ A budget for an event such as a school trip, holiday etc.

❗ A recording of daily or weekly sales of, say, a farm shop, a school shop, or a hamburger stand.

❗ The stock records of a small shop or sales outlet.

❗ Expenses such as mileage, accommodation, meals etc for a business user.

❗ Research on the Internet and a comparison of prices for goods or services such as computers, flights, etc. A record of these on a spreadsheet.

❗ A budget for a holiday.

❗ Average max and min temps for a holiday brochure (spreadsheet and chart).

Sample test questions

Questions 1 to 6 are based on Figure 1

A company records the expense claims made by their sales representatives.

	A	B	C	D	E	F
1		**Expense claims**				
2		February 2002				
3						
4	**Surname**	**Forename**	**Petrol**	**Meals**	**Total**	
5	Hale	Paul	£ 38.40	£ 20.50	£ 58.90	
6	Muir	Henry	£ 69.70	£ 45.00	£ 114.70	
7	Johns	Frances	£ 112.24	£ 65.50	£ 177.74	
8	Kent	Mary	£ 23.70	£ 10.50	£ 34.20	
9	Kashari	Abdul	£ 12.00	£ 7.50	£ 19.50	
10	Salam	Moya	£ 26.00	£ 15.00	£ 41.00	
11	Herbert	James	£ 15.89	£ 10.50	£ 26.39	
12	Attwood	Ken	£ 13.90	£ 10.50	£ 24.40	
13	Long	Sylvia	£ 120.78	£ 55.50	£ 176.28	
14	Grieg	Greta	£ 78.56	£ 30.50	£ 109.06	
15						
16						

Figure 1

1   Vertically, the spreadsheet is divided into:

A   rows

B   columns

C   bullets

D   tabs

2   Each item of data in the spreadsheet is entered in a:

A   square

B   toolbar

C   cell

D   formula

3   What formula should be entered in cell E15 to show the total value of the expense claims?

A   E5 to E14

B   =SUM(A15:D15)

C   =SUM(E5+E14)

D   =SUM(E5:E14)

4   The 'Petrol' column is formatted as:

A   number to 1 decimal place

B   date

C   integer

D   currency in pounds sterling

5   To make the column headings stand out, you could:

A   put a formula in cell A1

B   shade cells A4 to E4

C   put a border around cell A4

D   put a border around cell E15

6 Which person will be at the top of the list after sorting rows 5 to 14 on column 'A' in ascending order ?

A Moya Salam

B James Alderton

C Ken Attwood

D Frances Johns

Questions 7 – 8 are based on Figure 2

The following spreadsheet was produced to calculate the cost of decorating a room.

	A	B	C	D	E
1	Item	Item cost	Quantity	Item total	
2	Can of undercoat	£ 6.59	3		
3	Can of white gloss paint	£ 8.99	2		
4	Can of blue emulsion	£ 11.99	3		
5	Roll of wallpaper	£ 6.30	4		
6					

Figure 2

7 Which cell is selected in Figure 2?

A A1

B B2

C D2

D 7B

8 What formula is needed in cell D4 in order to calculate the cost of the blue emulsion required?

A B4xC4

B =B4:C4

C B4*C4

D =B4*C4

Questions 9 – 12 are based on Figure 3.

A local under-15's football league uses a spreadsheet to record their points. Each team is awarded 3 points for a win, 1 point for a draw and none for games they lose.

	A	B	C	D	E
1	Team	No. of games won	No. of games drawn	Total points	
2	Welton Wasps	5	0	15	
3	Burgoyne Falcons	3	1	10	
4	Melton Rangers	5	1	16	
5	Felston Town	5	2	17	
6	Wellington Eagles	2	3	9	
7	Greentown United	4	0	12	
8					

Figure 3

9 How many games have Wellington Eagles won?

    A   5

    B   3

    C   2

    D   4

10 To sort the teams into their positions in the league you would need to:

    A   sort on column A

    B   sort on row 7

    C   insert a column

    D   sort on column D

11 Which of these is the correct formula for cell D2?

    A   =(B2*3)+(C2*1)

    B   =(B2*1)+(C2*3)

    C   =(B2*3)-(C2*1)

    D   =(C2*3)-(B2*1)

12 Which one of the following charts shows the total points scored by each team?

    A   A

    B   B

    C   C

    D   D

A
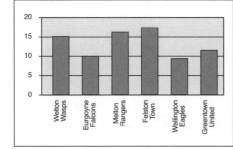

B
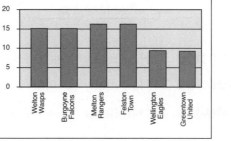

C
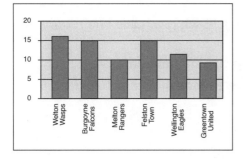

D
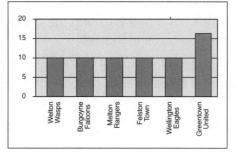

Chapter 6
Creating a Database

1

Databases are used to store large amounts of information. You can sort this information, often into alphabetical or numerical order, and select certain parts of the information to create useful reports.

For example, later in this chapter we will create a database of people who use Broomhill Sports Club. We might want to sort the database into alphabetic order of surname, or we might want to select all the people aged over 60 so that we can send them details of a new fitness class.

Information held in databases does not have to be just about people though, it can be about books, cars, hotels – in fact any items that you want to keep track of by recording specific details about them.

A database is based on **tables** of data, and each table contains many records (rows).

A **record** consists of many **fields.**

This is an example of a table of data:

Field name →

Field contents →

Equipment for hire	No. of items available	Hire cost (per hour)
Tennis racquet	12	£1.00
Badminton racquet	12	£0.50
Squash racquet	14	£2.00
Table tennis bat	10	£0.40

Table 1

Exercise 1: How many rows are there?

Exercise 2: How many columns are there?

Exercise 3: How many fields are there in each record?

Were you right?

There are 4 rows (not counting the headings). Each row holds one **record,** so there are 4 records in this table.

There are 3 columns. The column headings are the **field names.**

There are 3 fields in each record – the same as the number of columns.

The Sports Club can use this database to find out information such as:

- ! Whether or not they have a particular item for hire

- ! How many of a particular item they have

- ! How much it costs to hire a particular item

- ! Which is the most expensive item to hire

- ! Which items cost more than 50p to hire

Databases are not often used for such small amounts of data because answers to the above questions can easily be answered just by looking at the table. However, if you were a hire company and you had hundreds of items available for hire, the table would be so big it would take hours to answer the questions. This is when a database becomes very useful.

There are several different database programs available. The one used in this chapter is part of the **Microsoft Works** program.

Sample task

Create a database that records details of people who use Broomhill Sports Club

Designing the database

Some people are members of the club; others use 'Pay as you go'. For each person we want to store the following information:

- First name
- Surname
- Address line 1
- Address line 2
- Address line 3
- Address line 4
- Postcode

- Telephone no.
- Sex
- Age
- Registration date
- Member (Y or N)
- Type of membership

A record will be created for each person, made up of this list of fields. For some people certain fields may be left blank, for example if they only have three lines in their address. Address line 3 will always be used to hold the town name and Address line 4 will always be used to store the county name.

If a field has a choice of optional entries, it is often a good idea to have certain codes that can be entered instead of having to type in a lengthy description. For example we will just enter Y or N to indicate if a person is a member of the club. In Chapter 4 we created a table of Annual Membership Fees. Each type of membership needs a code. Table 2 shows the codes (in brackets) that will be entered.

	For one Person	Joint Membership	Family Membership
Full Membership	£250 (FullSingle)	£350 (FullJoint)	£400 (FullFamily)
Swimming only	£100 (SwimSingle)	£150 (SwimJoint)	£200 (SwimFamily)
Gym only	£125 (GymSingle)	£175 (GymJoint)	N/A
Sauna/Sunbed only	£75 (SSSingle)	£125 (SSJoint)	£150 (SSFamily)

Table 2

Tip:

Always separate first name and second name. This is so that you can sort alphabetically on surname.

Tip:

Always split the address into separate lines in case you want to find all the people that live in a particular county, for example.

Starting the database

▶ From the Windows desktop click **Start, Programs.**

▶ Click **Microsoft Works Database**.

Figure 6.1

▶ Click on **Blank Database** and then click **OK.**

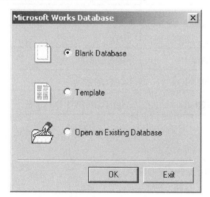

Figure 6.2

You will see the following dialogue box.

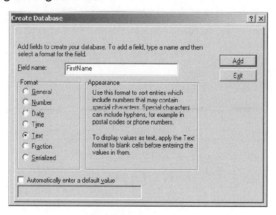

Figure 6.3

▶ In the Fieldname box type **FirstName.**

▶ Select the format **Text.**

▶ Click the **Add** button.

▶ Enter the remaining fields as shown below.

Description	Field name	Format
First name	FirstName	Text
Surname	LastName	Text
Address line 1	Address1	Text
Address line 2	Address2	Text
Address line 3	Address3	Text
Address line 4	Address4	Text
Postcode	Postcode	Text
Telephone No.	TelNo	Text
Age	Age	Number
Sex	Sex	Text
Registration date	RegDate	Date
Member? (Yes or No)	Member	Text
Type of membership	MembershipType	Text

Table 3

Tip:

Normally field names should not include spaces. Use capital letters in the middle of a field name to make the words easier to read.

▶ Click **Done.**

The empty database will be displayed.

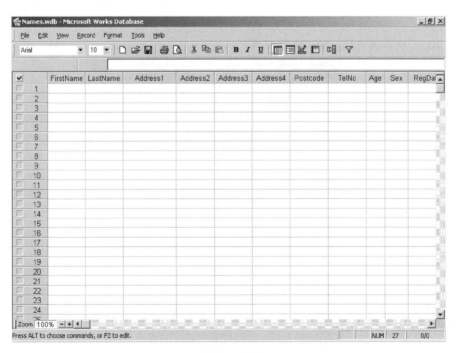

Figure 6.4

Editing the fields

You can change the width of any column by pointing at the right border of any column header (field name) until the cursor changes to a left- and right-pointing arrow (see Figure 6.5). Then drag to the left or right to make the column narrower or wider.

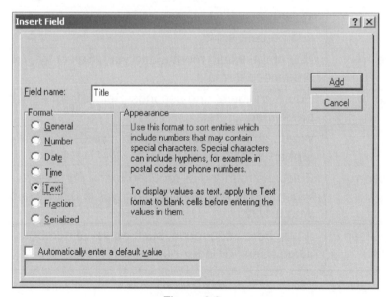

Figure 6.5

▶ Practise changing the widths of some of the columns.

If we decide that we should have included a field for the person's title e.g. Mr, Mrs etc. we can easily add a new field.

▶ Right-click the **FirstName** column header.

▶ Select **Insert Field, Before** from the shortcut menu.

▶ In the dialogue box enter the name of the new field **Title.**

Figure 6.6

▶ Click the **Add** button.

▶ Click the **Done** button.

A new column should appear in your database.

We can change the order of the fields by selecting the columns to be moved and dragging them.

Tip:
To delete a column simply right-click on the column header and select **Delete Field** from the shortcut menu.

▶ Click in the **Age** column header and drag across into the **Sex** column header.

▶ Drag the mouse pointer so that it points between the **LastName** and **Address1** fields.

The fields should have moved position.

Saving the database

▶ Save the database structure that you have created by pressing the **Save** button on the Standard toolbar or selecting **File, Save**.

▶ You will be asked to enter a file name for the database. Type the file name **Names** and click **Save**.

Field formats

When you created the database fields you chose a format from the list in the dialogue box (Figure 6.6). The table below explains what each of these formats means.

Type	Description
General	This is the default format. Uses integer (123) and decimal fraction (1.23).
Number	Numbers only with currency symbols, separators and percent signs.
Date	Day of the week, month, and year. Select from a list of predefined formats.
Time	Hours, minutes, and seconds. Select from a list of predefined formats.
Text	Words or information containing words and numbers i.e. **alphanumeric** data.
Fraction	Fractions rounded or reduced to the number you specify. When you type a fraction, first type a 0; for example, type **0 1/32**
Serialised	A numbered sequence, such as serial numbers, ID numbers, or index numbers.

Table 4

We will format the Age field to integer and the RegDate field to have the format dd/mm/yyyy (e.g. 13/02/2002).

▶ Click on the column header **Age**.

▶ Select **Format, Field**.

The Field name box will be displayed with several format options for **Age**.

Tip:

Integers are whole numbers with no decimal places.

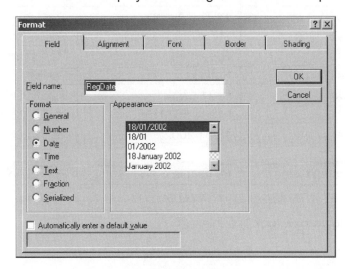

Figure 6.7

▶ Click on the top option **1234.56** and set the number of decimal places to **0**

▶ Click **OK.**

▶ Click on the column header **RegDate.**

▶ Select **Format, Field.**

The Field name box will be displayed showing several format options for **RegDate.**

Figure 6.8

▶ Click on the top option **18/01/2002.**

▶ Click **OK.** We will test this formatting when we enter some data.

▶ Save your work.

Tip:

Change views
by pressing the
buttons on
the toolbar.

Entering data

You can enter data in **List view,** which allows you to enter data into any field in any record. You are viewing the database in List view at the moment.

Alternatively you can enter data in **Form view,** which allows you to enter data for one record at a time.

▶ In List view, click in the first row of the **Title** column and type in **Mr.**

▶ Press the **Tab** key to move to the next field, or just click in the next field with the mouse.

▶ Type in **James.**

▶ Go to the **LastName** field and type **Kingsley.**

▶ Go to the **Age** field and type **25.**

▶ Complete this record and the next record with the details shown in Table 5.

Title	Mr	Miss
FirstName	James	Helen
Lastname	Kingsley	Burns
Age	25	35
Sex	M	F
Address1	14 The Avenue	The Limes
Address2		Green Road
Address3	Greenford	Marksham
Address4	Suffolk	Essex
Postcode	HJ71 6NM	YU67 9DF
TelNo	01234 567818	01456 223344
RegDate	18/01/2002	09/01/2002
Member	Y	Y
MembershipType	FullSingle	SwimSingle

Table 5

Your database should now look like this:

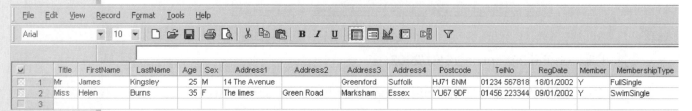

Figure 6.9

▶ Click the **Form View** button on the toolbar to enter two more records.

Because we moved some of the fields about, the form may look rather muddled. To rearrange the fields:

▶ Click the **Design View** button on the toolbar. ————————————

▶ Boxes will appear around each field label. Click on the one you want to move and drag it to a new position.

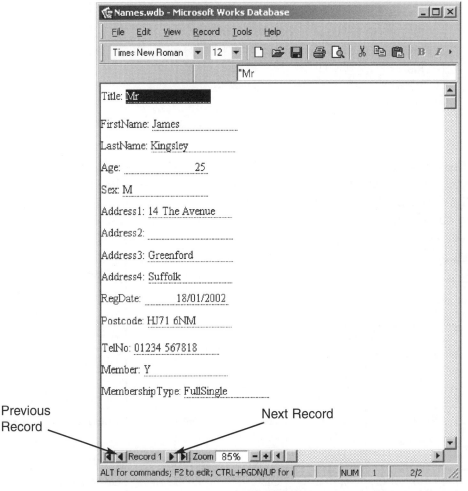

Figure 6.10

▶ In Form View use the **Next record** and **Previous record** arrows at the bottom of the window to move through the records until you get to the first blank one, which should be record 3.

▶ Click in the first field and type in the following two records. Use the **Tab** key to move between fields. When you reach the end of a record, pressing **Tab** will display a new blank record.

Chapter 6
Creating a Database

Title: Mr

FirstName: Harry

LastName: Carpenter

Age: 56

Sex: M

Address1: Bridge House

Address2:

Address3: East Harling

Address4: Essex

Postcode: CR56 8QW

TelNo: 01903 712341

RegDate: 14/06/2001

Member: Y

MembershipType: GymJoint

Title: Miss

FirstName: Jane

LastName: Highsmith

Age: 18

Sex: F

Address1: 45 High Street

Address2:

Address3: East Harling

Address4: Essex

Postcode: CR19 7GH

TelNo: 01903 675432

RegDate: 12/07/2001

Member: N

MembershipType:

Figure 6.11

Now enter the details of 6 more people (Table 6) either in List view or Form view, whichever you prefer. Remember that when entries are repeated like the address details for the Craig family (see Figure 6.12), you can use copy and paste to save typing in the same information over and over again. Remember to save your work.

Title	Mrs	Mr	Mr	Miss	Mr	Mr
FirstName	Sue	Barry	Sam	Kerry	Ashok	Ken
Lastname	Craig	Craig	Craig	Craig	Kanu	Jorgsen
Age	33	38	8	6	19	18
Sex	F	M	M	F	M	M
Address1	6 The Leys	6 The Leys	6 The Leys	6 The Leys	The Elms	Flat 6
Address2					Kings Walk	63, High St
Address3	West Harling	West Harling	West Harling	West Harling	Chelsfield	Marksham
Address4	Essex	Essex	Essex	Essex	Essex	Essex
Postcode	CR89 5FG	CR89 5FG	CR89 5FG	CR89 5FG	CK44 8VB	YU64 8JK
TelNo	01903 321987	01903 321987	01903 321987	01903 321987	01706 897651	01456 887766
RegDate	02/02/2000	02/02/2000	02/02/2000	02/02/2000	05/01/2001	21/11/2001
Member	Y	Y	Y	Y	N	N
Membership Type	FullFamily	FullFamily	FullFamily	FullFamily		

Table 6

In List View the database will now look like this:

		Title	FirstName	LastName	Age	Sex	Address1	Address2	Address3	Address4	Postcode	TelNo	RegDate	Member	MembershipType
	1	Mr	James	Kingsley	25	M	14 The Avenue		Greenford	Suffolk	HJ71 6NM	01234 567818	18/01/2002	Y	FullSingle
	2	Miss	Helen	Burns	35	F	The limes	Green Road	Marksham	Essex	YU67 9DF	01456 223344	09/01/2002	Y	SwimSingle
	3	Mr	Harry	Carpenter	56	M	Bridge House		East Harling	Essex	CR56 8QW	01903 712341	14/06/2001	Y	GymJoint
	4	Miss	Jane	Highsmith	18	F	45 High Street		East Harling	Essex	CR19 7GH	01903 675432	12/07/2001	N	
	5	Mrs	Sue	Craig	33	F	6 The Leys		West Harling	Essex	CR89 5FG	01903 321987	02/02/2000	Y	FullFamily
	6	Mr	Barry	Craig	38	M	6 The Leys		West Harling	Essex	CR89 5FG	01903 321987	02/02/2000	Y	FullFamily
	7	Mr	Sam	Craig	8	M	6 The Leys		West Harling	Essex	CR89 5FG	01903 321987	02/02/2000	Y	FullFamily
	8	Miss	Kerry	Craig	6	F	6 The Leys		West Harling	Essex	CR89 5FG	01903 321987	02/02/2000	Y	FullFamily
	9	Mr	Ashok	Kanu	19	M	The Elms	Kings Walk	Chelsfield	Essex	CK44 8VB	01706 897651	05/01/2001	N	
	10	Mr	Ken	Jorgsen	18	M	Flat 6	63, High Street	Marksham	Essex	YU64 8JK	01456 887766	21/11/2001	N	

Figure 6.12

Hundreds of people use Broomhill Sports Club. We have entered the details of only a few of them here.

Editing data

You can change the contents of any field by clicking in the field and editing in the normal way. Use the **Backspace** or **Delete** key to delete unwanted text and type the corrections.

You can undo changes by selecting **Edit, Undo.**

Sorting records

Suppose you want to sort the database records into alphabetical order of surname.

▶ Select **Record, Sort Records.**

▶ In the Sort Records window choose to sort by **LastName** and then (if two or more people have the same surname) by **FirstName.**

▶ Click the **Ascending** option for both fields.

▶ Click **OK.**

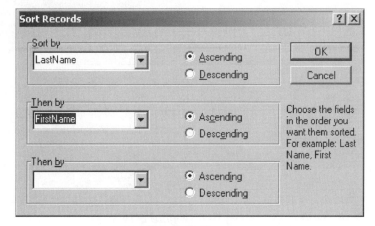

Figure 6.13

The sorted table will be displayed in List View.

Chapter 6
Creating a Database

Querying the database

One of the most useful things you can do with a database is to find all the records that satisfy a certain condition, such as all the people that live in Marksham. We call this a **query** or a **filter.**

▶ Click the **Filters** button on the toolbar.

▶ In the Filter window that appears (see Figure 6.15) click on **Rename Filter.**

▶ In the Filter Name box type in a name such as **Marksham.**

Figure 6.14

▶ Click **OK.**

▶ Back in the Filter window click the **Easy Filter** option at the top.

▶ Use the down arrow to select the Field name **Address3.**

▶ Use the next down arrow to select the Comparison **is equal to.**

▶ In the Compare To box type in **Marksham.**

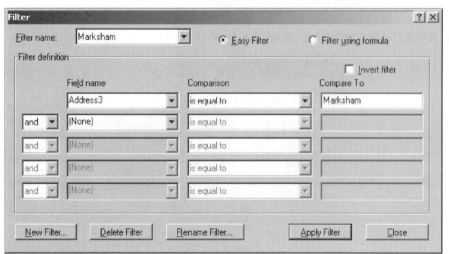

Figure 6.15

Tip:

Here you are selecting all the records that have the word Marksham in the field Address3. Now you can see why it was important that we always put the town in Address3.

▶ Click **Apply Filter.**

Your database will reappear displaying only those people who live in Marksham.

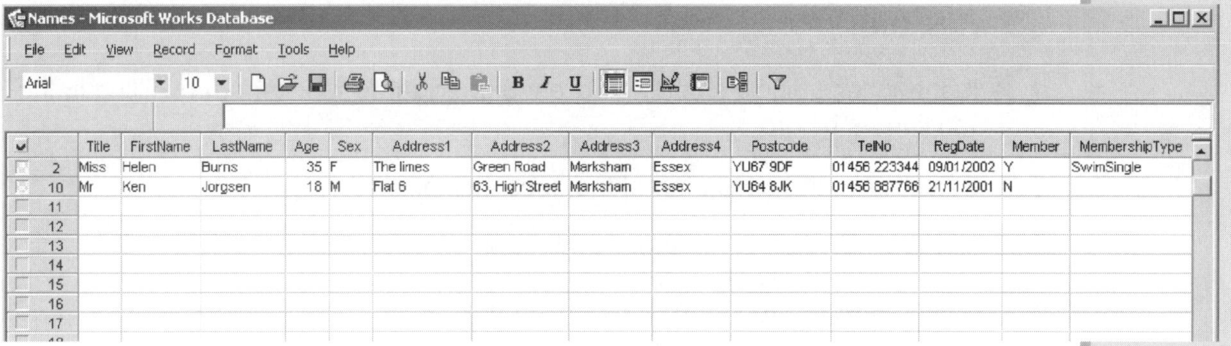

Figure 6.16

Comparison symbols

As you have seen, in Microsoft Works database the comparisons are written in words. In some other databases, these are written as symbols (or **operators**).

Symbol	Meaning	Example
<	Less than	<50
<=	Less than or equal to	<=50
>	Greater than	>10
>=	Greater than or equal to	>=10
=	Equal to	=10 =Marksham OR East Harling
<>	Not equal to	<>Chelmsford
BETWEEN	Test for a range of values	Between 01/02/2001 AND 10/12/2001

Table 7

Notice the use of the words **OR** and **AND** in the examples in the third column of the above table. These can be used to make the comparison more detailed.

We can find all the people who live in Marksham OR East Harling, but it would not be sensible to look for all the people who live in Marksham AND East Harling because Address3 cannot be equal to both.

▶ Select **Record**, **Show**, **All Records**, to bring all the records back on the screen.

▶ Click the **Filters** button.

▶ Click **New Filter**.

▶ Enter a name such as **Marksham or EH**.

▶ Click **OK**.

▶ In the Filter window specify **Address3 is equal to Marksham** by filling in the top line as before.

▶ Select **or** at the beginning of the second line.

▶ Select **Address3** in the Field name box.

▶ Select **is equal to** in the Comparison box.

▶ Type in **East Harling** in the Compare To box.

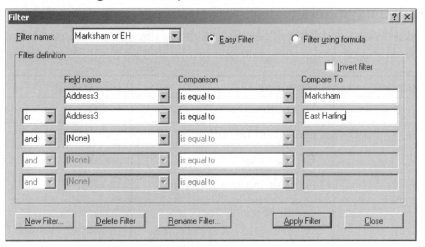

Figure 6.17

▶ Click **Apply Filter**.

The database will display only those people who live in either Marksham or East Harling.

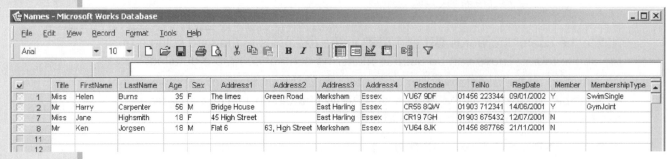

		Title	FirstName	LastName	Age	Sex	Address1	Address2	Address3	Address4	Postcode	TelNo	RegDate	Member	MembershipType
	1	Miss	Helen	Burns	35	F	The limes	Green Road	Marksham	Essex	YU67 9DF	01456 223344	09/01/2002	Y	SwimSingle
	2	Mr	Harry	Carpenter	56	M	Bridge House		East Harling	Essex	CR56 8QW	01903 712341	14/06/2001	Y	GymJoint
	7	Miss	Jane	Highsmith	18	F	45 High Street		East Harling	Essex	CR19 7GH	01903 675432	12/07/2001	N	
	8	Mr	Ken	Jorgsen	18	M	Flat 6	63, High Street	Marksham	Essex	YU64 8JK	01456 887766	21/11/2001	N	
	11														
	12														

Figure 6.18

▶ Save your work.

Exercise 4: Show all the database records, sort on age (ascending) and create a query to select all the females in the database.

Sample Assignment

Background

You are asked to produce a database for the Head Office of a company that has retail outlets around the UK and Ireland. In the table below, the stores are organised by area.

Branch number	Branch name	Tel. no.	No. of staff	Branch Manager		Opening date
				Surname	Forename	
Central London						
117	Marble Arch	020 889 1234	42	Dent	Jane	09/03/01
377	Swiss Cottage	020 834 1789	29	Raj	Sanjit	08/01/98
221	Kensington	020 867 1890	52	Kirby	Robert	04/11/97
480	Oxford Street	020 845 1567	55	Hutchins	John	01/06/99
England						
403	Basildon	01268 167891	35	Fletcher	Marie	02/10/00
429	Chester	01244 123412	33	Jones	Gita	02/10/00
251	Doncaster	01302 897651	37	Davies	Alastair	08/01/98
531	Canterbury	01227 890156	34	Lee	Brian	04/12/00
160	Loughborough	01509 876781	33	Wynberg	Ian	16/03/00
061	Bournemouth	01202 987678	38	Derbyshire	Rosie	28/07/01
017	Leeds	0113 881188	39	Mellor	Alex	12/10/99
Wales						
296	Bangor	01248 222999	27	Johns	Mary	15/09/01
050	Swansea	01792 765456	25	Hill	Dave	12/12/98
Scotland						
112	Glasgow	0141 121671	24	McCree	Hugh	12/12/98
538	Edinburgh	0131 836423	24	Major	David	27/02/99
Northern Ireland						
466	Belfast	028 813 45211	26	Blaines	Steve	09/11/98
088	Newry	028 302 82451	25	Leggett	Sunita	07/03/00

Chapter 6
Creating a Database

Tasks

1   In a database package set up a table with the following fields:

Field name	Data type
Branch number	Text
Area	Text
Branch name	Text
Tel. no.	Text
No. of staff	Number (integer)
Manager surname	Text
Manager forename	Text
Opening date	Date

2   Save your file with a suitable filename and print the table.

3   A new branch has opened. Enter its details:

   Cambridge, Telephone no. 012226 67345, Branch no. 325, 44 staff, Manager James Drew, Opening date 12/02/02.

4   The Basildon store has a new manager named Francis Harding. Amend the record accordingly.

5   Sort the database into alphabetical order (ascending) of branch name. Print the table again.

6   Query the database to find all stores with more than 35 staff. Print out the results of this query.

7   Use Print Screen to print a screenshot of Windows Explorer showing where your database is saved.

8   On a separate piece of paper answer the following questions:

   • How many fields does your database have?

   • How many records does your database have?

   • What advantages does a computerised database like this one have over a manual system?

   • Why is the data type integer number used for the field **No. of staff**?

Evidence to collect

   • Printout for task 2.

   • Printout for task 5.

   • Printout for task 6.

   • Printout for task 7.

   • The answers to task 8 on a separate sheet of paper.

Relating the assignment to the specification

Specification Reference (Part B)	What has been done to satisfy this
IT1.1	
• Find and select relevant information.	• Task 1
• Enter and bring in information, using formats that help development.	• Tasks 1, 3, 4 and 5
• Explore and develop information to meet your purpose.	• Task 6
IT1.2	
• Use appropriate layouts for presenting information in a consistent way.	• Tasks 1, 2, 3, 4, 5 and 6
• Develop the presentation so that it is accurate, clear and meets your purpose.	• Tasks 1-8
• Save information so that it can be found easily.	• Tasks 2 and 7

Other Key Skills signposting

Communication C1.3.

Ideas for other assignments

- A database of cars for sale at a car auction in which the user can look up records of cars in a certain price range.

- A database of houses for sale in which the user can look up all properties that suit their requirements.

- A database of a squash ladder at a Sports Club showing the position of people in the ladder.

- A database of your CD/DVD collection.

- A database of hotels in your local area in which a user can look up all hotels with certain facilities.

Chapter 6
Creating a Database

Sample test questions

Questions 1-5 are based on Figure 1

An evening class tutor wants to store information about her students. The information is shown in the table below.

Surname	Forename	Tel. Number	Age
Akaly	Mohammed	01235 567845	28
Brown	George	01912 898989	35
Mahali	Saloni	01237 123423	41
Marshall	Sue	01912 123458	25
Bence	Matt	01654 987653	29
Dutoit	Pierre	01932 678933	40

Figure 1

1   The best way to store these details would be to use a:

A   web browser

B   database

C   accounts package

D   graphics program

2   To find all the people over the age of 30 requires a search for:

A   Age $\neq$ 30

B   Age < 30

C   Age = 30

D   Age > 30

3   The information shown contains:

A   4 files, 6 records

B   6 fields, 4 records

C   4 fields, 6 records

D   6 fields, 4 records

4   To put the students in alphabetical order of name in the database requires a:

A   revision

B   search

C   query

D   sort

5   The entries for Tel. Number should be of type:

A   numeric

B   text

C   integer

D   Yes/No

Questions 6 - 9 refer to Figure 2

A bookshop holds records of the following books in a database.

Title	Author	Category	Price	No. in stock
Databases in Easy Lessons	J. King	Adult non-fiction	£9.99	4
The Night of the Yearlings	H.J. Lemming	Adult fiction	£6.49	3
Henry's First Cake	F. Burton	Child fiction	£4.99	2
The Saints of the Crypt	B. Marling	Adult fiction	£5.99	2
Advanced Maths Problems	K. Ormerod	Adult non-fiction	£15.99	1
Sky boy	S. Shaw	Adult fiction	£7.99	3
Art on Record	T. Taylor	Adult non-fiction	£20.99	2
Tales to Chill	G. Trip	Child fiction	£3.99	3

Figure 2

6 The information on 'Sky boy' is in record number:

    A   1

    B   3

    C   6

    D   7

7 Which book would appear first when the data is sorted in ascending order of Price?

    A   Advanced Maths Problems

    B   Tales to Chill

    C   Art on Record

    D   Databases in Easy Lessons

8 Details of books in the Adult non-fiction category can be found in the database using:

    A   Category > "Adult non-fiction"

    B   Category < "Adult non-fiction"

    C   Category = "Adult non-fiction"

    D   Category ≠ "Child fiction"

9 In this database **Author** is a:

    A   database record

    B   data type

    C   row name

    D   field name

Chapter 6
Creating a Database

Questions 10 – 14 refer to Figure 3

A vet's surgery keeps the following database of dogs who have visited the practice.

Name	Breed	Date of last vaccination	Owner's name	Tel. Number
Sophie	West Highland terrier	27/02/01	Richards	01256 783451
Rockie	Afghan hound	12/05/01	Major	01235 678988
Rover	German shepherd	09/01/00	Church	01346 784531
Doc	Mongrel	18/12/01	Derbyshire	01346 142322
Jet	Black labrador	08/09/00	Lee	01256 991231
Maisie	Cocker spaniel	01/02/02	Farthing	01235 444521

Figure 3

10 How many fields are there in each record in the database?

A   8

B   9

C   5

D   6

11 In this database, **Breed** is a:

A   database record

B   data type

C   row name

D   field name

12 The telephone number for the owner of Rockie is:

A   01346 142322

B   01235 678988

C   01235 444521

D   01256 783451

13 To find all the dogs who have been vaccinated since February last year, you would need to search:

A   the **Name** field

B   the **Date of last vaccination** field

C   the **Tel. Number** field

D   every field in the database

14 If the vet wanted to add a new dog called Whiskey to the database, he would have to:

A   add a new field

B   rename a field

C   delete another dog from the database

D   add a new record

Part 2

Application of Number

(2)

Chapter 7
Interpreting Information

Read and understand tables

A table is a quick and easy way to present information. It consists of columns and rows with headings and labels.

Look at the first three columns of a table we used in an earlier chapter.

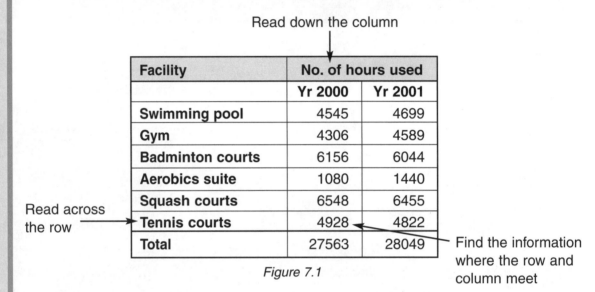

Read down the column

Facility	No. of hours used	
	Yr 2000	Yr 2001
Swimming pool	4545	4699
Gym	4306	4589
Badminton courts	6156	6044
Aerobics suite	1080	1440
Squash courts	6548	6455
Tennis courts	4928	4822
Total	27563	28049

Read across the row

Find the information where the row and column meet

Figure 7.1

Reading information from the table is easy: find the row you want, then the column you want, and the information will be found where the two cross.

For example, if we want to know how many hours the tennis courts were used for in the year 2000, we would look across the **Tennis courts** row and down the **Yr 2000** column – where they meet will hold the answer (i.e. 4928).

Exercise 1: How many hours was the gym used for in 2001?

Exercise 2: What was the total number of hours the facilities were used for in 2000?

Of course tables can have lots more rows and columns. Let's add two more columns to our table. One shows the average number of hours over the two years and the final column shows the amount of money, or revenue, made from each of the facilities over the two years.

Facility	No. of hours used		Average	Revenue
	Yr 2000	Yr 2001		
Swimming pool	4545	4699	4622	£ 110,306
Gym	4306	4589	4448	£ 111,200
Badminton courts	6156	6044	6100	£ 12,200
Aerobics suite	1080	1440	1260	£ 63,000
Squash courts	6548	6455	6502	£ 22,757
Tennis courts	4928	4822	4875	£ 24,375
Total	27563	28049		£ 343,838

Figure 7.2

Exercise 3: Can you see how much money was made from Aerobics?

Exercise 4: Which facility made the least amount of money?

Exercise 5: Did the squash courts generate more revenue than the tennis courts?

Sometimes when you are working with large numbers like these it is easier to read the information from a chart or graph. These will be covered in the following sections.

Reading and understanding charts

Pie Charts

In Chapter 5 the revenue made from the different facilities was shown in a pie chart. A pie chart is used to show the amount each value contributes to the whole. So a piece of the 'pie' shown below represents how much money one particular activity contributes to the total.

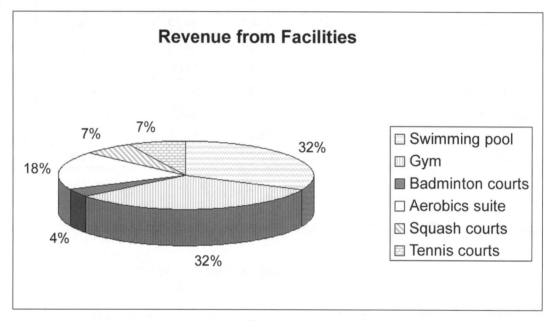

Figure 7.3

We can see that the swimming pool and the gym generated the most revenue – 32% each in fact which as you can see from the pie chart is getting on for one third of the total revenue each.

Sometimes pie charts are labelled with the exact values i.e. the swimming pool sector would be labelled £110,306 instead of 32%. Because of lack of space the sectors of a pie chart are often colour-coded and a legend shows which sector represents which item. Because the pie chart above is printed in black and white, patterns have been used to distinguish each sector.

Exercise 6: What percentage of total revenue was generated from the aerobics suite?

Exercise 7: What percentage of total revenue was generated from the squash courts and the badminton courts together?

Bar Charts

Bar charts are another way of presenting information that is easy to read. In Chapter 5, a bar chart was produced to compare the numbers of hours that different facilities were used in the year 2000 and the year 2001. Sometimes only one set of numbers would be used, e.g. just one year. Because this chart has two sets of data, a legend is used again to let us know which bars represent which year.

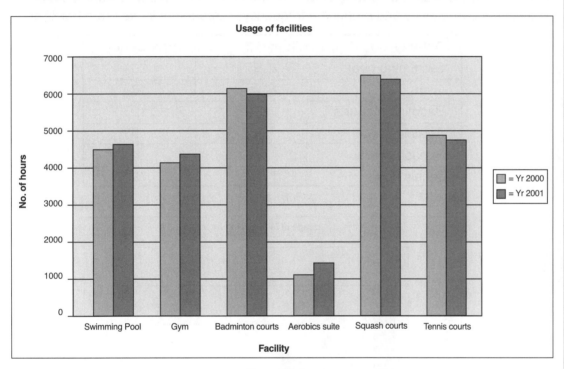

Figure 7.4

Tip:
Sometimes the bars are shown horizontally instead of vertically.

The scale at the left-hand side allows you to read off values. This chart allows you to compare the usage of the different facilities between the two years. For example we can see that in 2000 the least used facility was the aerobics suite. We can also see that in 2001 the use of the aerobics suite increased.

Exercise 8: Which facility was used the most in the year 2000?

Exercise 9: Which facilities were used less in 2001 than in 2000?

Reading and understanding diagrams

Frequency diagrams

When information is collected from, for example, a survey, the number of times a particular measurement occurs is called the frequency. If we wanted to do a survey of the facilities people came to use at the Sports Club during one particular hour we could record the results on a **tally chart.** At the end of the hour-long survey we can calculate the frequency and produce a frequency diagram that looks like a bar chart.

Activity	Tally	Frequency
Swimming pool	ⅢⅢ ⅢⅢ ⅢⅢ ⅢⅢ	20
Gym	ⅢⅢ ⅢⅢ ⅢⅢ	16
Badminton courts	ⅢⅢ ⅢⅢ ||	12
Aerobics suite		0
Squash courts	||||	4
Tennis courts	ⅢⅢ |||	8

Figure 7.5

> **Tip:**
> To draw a tally chart make a stroke for each person. The fifth stroke is slanted to finish a number group.

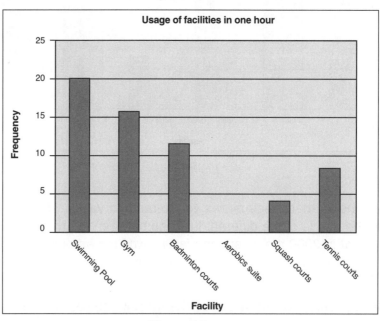

Figure 7.6

So, in this case the frequency is simply the total number that came to the club to use a particular facility.

Exercise 10: Which facility was the most popular?

Exercise 11: Which facility was least popular?

Exercise 12: Do you think it is easier to tell this from the tally chart or the frequency diagram?

Pictograms

A pictogram is quite a fun type of chart. It uses pictures or symbols to show how many items fall into a particular category.

Usually one picture counts for more than one item. We could use a pictogram to show how many people used the facilities on a particular day. One smiley face stands for 10 people – so half a smiley face stands for 5 people.

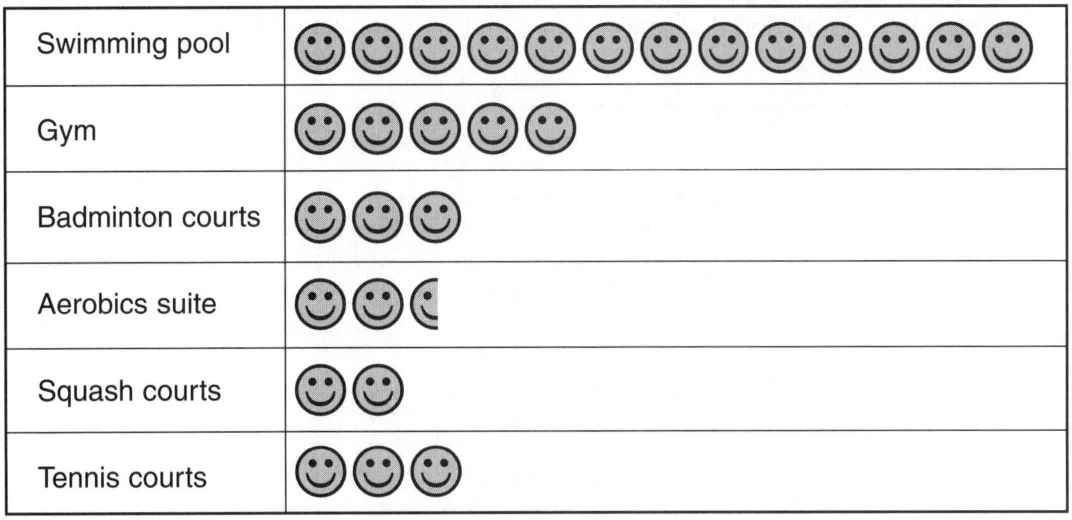

Swimming pool	☺☺☺☺☺☺☺☺☺☺☺☺☺
Gym	☺☺☺☺☺
Badminton courts	☺☺☺
Aerobics suite	☺☺◖
Squash courts	☺☺
Tennis courts	☺☺☺

Figure 7.7

From the pictogram we can see that 50 people used the gym on that day.

Exercise 13: How many people attended aerobics classes?

Exercise 14: If we decide that one smiley face is equal to 15 people, how many people used the gym?

Exercise 15: Did more people play squash or play tennis?

Read and understand line graphs

A graph shows how two different quantities relate to each other. The numbers are laid out on the X-axis along the bottom and the Y-axis down the side. The relationship between the numbers is shown by a continuous line.

Line graphs can be useful to convert from one unit to another. For example at the Sports Club the temperature of different areas of the building is very important. Staff need to be able to convert between Fahrenheit and Celsius. A table would allow them to read off certain temperatures, but a chart allows them to read off any temperature.

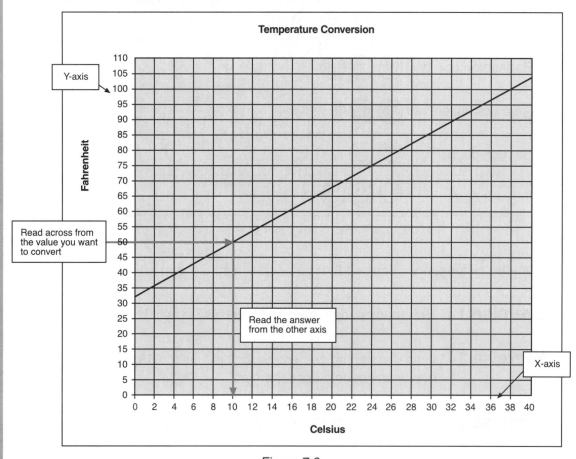

Figure 7.8

To convert, for example 50 degrees Fahrenheit into Celsius, read across from 50 on the Y-axis until you meet the line, then drop down and read the answer from the X-axis – the equivalent temperature is 10 degrees Celsius.

Exercise 16: If instructions for the sauna say that it should be maintained at a temperature of 40 degrees Celsius, what is the equivalent temperature in Fahrenheit?

Expressing a number in different ways

If you look back at the table in Figure 7.2 and the pie chart in Figure 7.3 you can see that the revenue made from different activities is shown in two different ways – in the table it is shown as pounds and in the pie chart as percentages.

Let's think about the numbers in the table first – here it is again:

Facility	No. of hours used		Average	Revenue
	Yr 2000	**Yr 2001**		
Swimming pool	4545	4699	4622	£ 110,306
Gym	4306	4589	4448	£ 111,200
Badminton courts	6156	6044	6100	£ 12,200
Aerobics suite	1080	1440	1260	£ 63,000
Squash courts	6548	6455	6502	£ 22,757
Tennis courts	4928	4822	4875	£ 24,375
Total	27563	28049		£ 343,838

Figure 7.9

There are only ten basic digits in our number system: 0, 1, 2, 3, 4, 5, 6, 7, 8, 9, but these can be combined together to make very large numbers.

Large numbers

If you have a lot of digits, they are often put into groups of three with a space or a comma between the groups. Look at the **Revenue** column in the table above and you can see that the numbers have been separated with commas. It is also important to line up the decimal points in this kind of column.

You have to be able to write numbers in words as well as in figures. In the table above, the total revenue is shown as £343,838. This would be written as

three hundred and forty three thousand, eight hundred and thirty eight.

Exercise 17: How would you write the revenue from the squash courts in words?

Exercise 18: Which facility generated revenue of twelve thousand and two hundred pounds?

Fractions, decimals and percentages

Sometimes numbers need to show part of a whole. This is where fractions, decimals and percentages come in.

You will recognise some of the common ones:

	Fraction	Decimal	Percentage
One-tenth	$^1/_{10}$	0.1	10%
One-quarter	$^1/_4$	0.25	25%
One-half	$^1/_2$	0.5	50%
Three-quarters	$^3/_4$	0.75	75%

In the next chapter you will practise calculating fractions, decimals and percentages. It is often useful, though, to remember the ones in the table above. Memorising these can help you to estimate other percentages, or calculate decimals accurately.

Exercise 19: What is 50% as a fraction?

What is $^3/_4$ as a decimal?

What is 0.25 as a fraction?

What is 50% of 200?

What is $^1/_4$ of 16?

Measuring in everyday units

Quantities or amounts are measured in different units depending on what is being measured. You need to be familiar with the units that are used to measure everyday quantities.

Sometimes you have a choice of units to use – the metric system (metres, litres, grams) is the official system of measurement in most countries, but the imperial system (feet, pints and pounds) is still often used in the UK and the USA.

Here are some common metric units and what they are used for:

Length	Unit	Symbol
	Millimetre	mm
	Centimetre	cm
	Metre	m
	Kilometre	km

Remember:

10mm = 1cm

100cm = 1m

1000m = 1km

Exercise 20: Approximately how wide is the book?

How many metres is 265cm?

How many centimetres is 45mm?

Weight	Unit	Symbol
	Milligram	mg
	Gram	g
	Kilogram	kg

Remember:

1000mg = 1g

1000g = 1kg

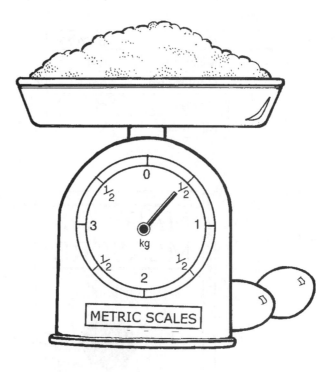

Exercise 21: Approximately how much flour is being weighed?

How many milligrams is 4.5g?

How many grams is 2500mg?

How many kilograms is 1750g?

How many grams is 2kg?

Volume (liquids)	Unit	Symbol
	Millilitre	ml
	Litre	l

Remember:

1000ml = 1l

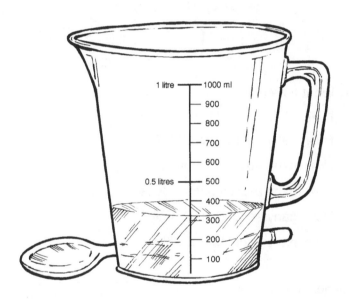

Exercise 22: Approximately how much milk is there?

How many litres would 4700ml be?

How many ml would 3.2l be?

Chapter 7
Interpreting Information

Time	Unit	Symbol
	Millisecond	ms
	Second	s
	Minute	min
	Hour	hr

Remember:
1000ms = 1s
60s = 1min
60min = 1hr

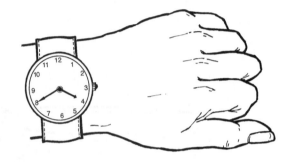

Exercise 23: What time is it?

How many seconds is 1500ms?

How many minutes is 180s?

How many hours is 150min?

How many milliseconds is 2.5s?

How many seconds is 4.5min?

How many minutes is 3.25hr?

Some digital watches and clocks and many countries overseas use the **24-hour clock**. This means you do not have to specify am or pm.

Time is expressed as a 4-digit number. The first two digits indicate the hour and the second two digits represent the minute. The hours are numbered from 00 through to 23, with midnight = 00. Minutes are shown from 01 through to 59.

Examples:

24-hour clock	12-hour clock
0000	12.00am (midnight)
0230	2.30am
0505	5.05am
1200	12.00pm (noon)
1435	2.35pm
2258	10.58pm

Exercise 24: What would 9 o'clock in the evening be on the 24hr clock?

What would 1 o'clock in the afternoon be on the 24hr clock?

What would 16.30 be on a non-digital watch?

What would 20.00 be on a non-digital watch?

Temperature	Unit	Symbol
	Celsius	°C

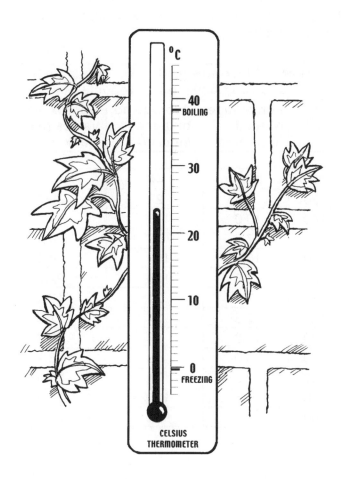

Exercise 25: How hot is it?

Identify suitable calculations to get the results you need

You should already be familiar with the most common types of calculations including addition, subtraction, multiplication and division.

When you read information from tables and charts or measure quantities and amounts you may be asked to perform these types of calculations on the data you collect. You should know how to pick out the calculation you need for a task e.g. I need to *multiply* these two numbers together or I need to *subtract* this number from the other one. The Sample Assignment will give you some practice.

Sample Assignment

Background

The manager of your local Novus supermarket has asked you to help him analyse some data about the store and to undertake some research for him. He provides you with the following information.

Novus: Floor space, turnover and staffing (foods and household products only)						
Section	Area (m²)	Percentage of total floor area	Average no. of items stocked	Approx. sales values per week in £000	Staff allocated to section	
					Male	Female
*Vegetables	200	12.5	46	28.3	1	1
*Fruit	120	7.5	29	33.2	1	
Canned foods	160	10.0	116	17.5		1
Bread and cakes	120	7.5	58	20.4		1
**Dairy	160	10.0	102	14.1	1	2
Alcoholic drinks	120	7.5	128	22.7	2	
Soft drinks	120	7.5	34	17.6	1	
**Meats	120	7.5	34	17.6	2	1
***Frozen foods	240	15.0	87	20.2	1	2
Cereals	80	5.0	48	8.7		1
Pet foods	40	2.5	74	14.8		1
Household	120	7.5	126	16.5		1
TOTAL	1600		924	233.3	9	11

*   Chilled areas

**   Superchilled areas

*** Frozen areas

The remaining areas are at general store temperature.

Tasks

Read the table of data and answer the following questions:

1   What is the average number of items stocked in the **Canned foods** section?

2   How many people work in the **Dairy** section?

3   What floor space is allocated to the **Pet foods** section?

4   What percentage of the total floor space is allocated to the **Household** section?

5   What is the approximate weekly sales value of the **Soft drinks** section? Write this amount in words.

6   Which sections are superchilled?

7   What calculation would you perform to find out how many staff are responsible for the **Fruit** and **Vegetable** sections together?

8   What calculation would you perform to find the total average number of items stocked in the sections which are at general store temperature?

9   The general manager wishes to know by how much the total weekly value of sales in the **Fruit** and **Vegetable** sections combined exceeds the total of the **Alcoholic drinks** and **Soft drinks** sections combined. What calculations would you perform to give him the answer?

10   What calculation would you need to do to find out the average area supervised by each member of staff in the **Meats** section?

11   The recommended temperature for superchilled foods is in the range of $1^{O}C$ to $3^{O}C$. Find out the approximate Fahrenheit (^{O}F) equivalents.

12   The width of the shelves in the **Pet foods** section is 1.2m. What is the equivalent of this in centimetres?

13   Staff must arrive at the store by ten to nine in the morning. Draw a clock face to show where the hands would be pointing at this time.

14   The staff can leave at 1735. Draw a clock face to show where the hands would be pointing at this time.

Finally, visit your local supermarket and look at the items on the shelves and cabinets.

15   What items are shown with weights in grams?

16   What items are shown in litres? This is a measure of what?

17   In which section(s) are prices shown in both £.p. per kg (kilogram) and £.p. per lb (pound)? Record examples of these.

Evidence to collect

•   Answers to tasks 1 – 14, neatly presented and showing your working.

•   Details of which supermarket you visited and the information you collected for tasks 15 – 17.

Relating the assignment to the specification

Specification Reference (Part B)	What has been done to satisfy this
N1.1	
• Obtain the information you need to meet the purpose of your task.	• Tasks 1 – 6, 11 – 17
• Identify suitable calculations to get the results you need.	• Tasks 7 – 10
N1.2	
• Carry out calculations to the levels of accuracy you have been given.	
• Check your results make sense.	
N1.3	
• Choose suitable ways to present your findings.	
• Present your findings clearly.	
• Describe how the results of your calculations meet the purposes of your task	

Ideas for other assignments

! Analysis of the results of science experiments represented by tables and charts.

! Analysis of newspaper reports that include charts or tables on current news topics such as crime rates, population growth, global warming etc.

! Analysis of company performance from an Annual Report that contains tables and charts.

Sample test questions

1 Four students measure their height.

Haj is measured first.

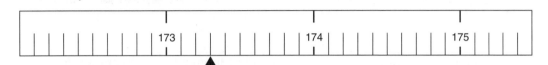

How much does Haj measure?

A   1m 73.3cm

B   176cm

C   1m 733cm

D   733cm

2 The other students also measure themselves and write down their heights in a chart but they don't all use the same units.

Name	Height
Sandy	1640mm
Marina	1m 58cm
Gregor	1m 74cm
Toby	177cm

Which is the tallest student?

A   Haj

B   Toby

C   Marina

D   Gregor

3 How much taller than Marina is Sandy?

A   40mm

B   14cm

C   0.6m

D   0.06m

4 Abdullah arrives at Ipswich station at 10 past 1 in the afternoon. He catches the next train to London. Here is the timetable:

Ipswich	Manningtree	Colchester	London
1300	1309	1320	1415
1314	--------	1331	1420
1330	1339	1349	1438
1341	1352	1402	1452
1400	1409	1420	1515

What time does he arrive in London?

A   1452

B   1420

C   1331

D   1438

5   If he decides not to go to London, but just to Manningtree, which train from Ipswich should he catch to get there the quickest?

A   1314

B   1341

C   1330

D   1339

6   If the 1400 train from Ipswich is delayed by 10 minutes, what time will it arrive in London?

A   1515

B   1535

C   Twenty five minutes past 5

D   Twenty five minutes past 3

A netball league keeps a record of the number of goals scored each season.
The pictogram shows how many goals they scored in the 2001 season.

Helston Heights	★★★★★
Ipswich Majors	★★★
Kelsale Town	★★★
Merton Minors	★★
Clapton Comrades	★★★
Heathtown Ladies	★★★★
Burton NC	★★★★

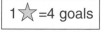
1 ★ =4 goals

7   How many goals did Kelsale Town score?

A   8

B   3

C   10

D   6

8   How many goals were scored in the league altogether?

A   86

B   96

C   90

D   80

This is the information on the side of a 600g box of corn flakes.

Nutritional content	One 30g serving provides
Energy	1650kj / 390kcal
Protein	6.0g
Carbohydrates	83.0g
Fat	3.5g
Fibre	2.6g
Sodium	0.7g

9 How much fat is there in half a box (300g) of cornflakes?

A   2.5g

B   3.5g

C   25.0g

D   35.0g

10 All the amounts in the table (except for Energy) are given to the nearest

A   ten grams

B   gram

C   hundreth of a gram

D   tenth of a gram

11 A school is given a lottery grant for a new gym. The school newsletter carries the following headline:

Work can now start on our new quarter of a million pound gym

How much is this in figures?

A   £25,000

B   £250,000

C   £2,500,000

D   £400,000

12 If a child has a bag containing 36 sweets and he gives 9 away, how many of his original sweets has he left?

A $^1/_4$

B $^3/_4$

C   one half

D   25%

13 What does a tally chart measure?

A   height

B   train times

C   width

D   frequency

Chapter 8
Calculations

Common calculations

The most common calculations that we carry out in everyday life include the following:

Add	+
Subtract (take away)	-
Multiply (times)	x
Divide	÷

Exercise 1: Without using a calculator can you do the following?

19 + 6	=
17 + 11	=
27 – 12	=
33 – 10	=
6 x 12	=
2 x 27	=
55 ÷ 5	=
18 ÷ 3	=

You will often use a calculator to perform calculations, but there are still some simple rules you need to remember.

Order of calculation

Sometimes you will be asked to work out a calculation that has several different parts to it and you may not be sure which bit to do first.

For example, if you were given the following calculation you would get a different answer depending on whether you did the addition or the multiplication first.

$5 + 6 \times 2 = 22$ if you do the addition first, the answer will be **incorrect**

$5 + 6 \times 2 = 17$ if you do the multiplication first, the answer will be **correct**

Brackets may be used to keep parts of the calculation together. Always do the part of the calculation in the brackets first.

$5 + (6 \times 2) = 17$

There is a word that you can memorise which will help you to remember the correct order for doing all calculations:

BODMAS

B	Brackets
O	Other (operations such as 2^2)
D	Division
M	Multiplication
A	Addition
S	Subtraction

Using this rule we can see that:

Example 1:

$6 + 3 \times 2 - 8 \div 2$	$=$	$6 + 3 \times 2 - 4$
	$=$	$6 + 6 - 4$
	$=$	$12 - 4$
	$=$	8

Division first
Multiplication next
Addition next
Subtraction last

Example 2:

$6 \times (4 + 5) - 8 + 6$	$=$	$6 \times 9 - 8 + 6$
	$=$	$54 - 8 + 6$
	$=$	$54 - 14$
	$=$	40

Brackets first
Multiplication next
Addition next
Subtraction last

Example 3:

$(2 \times 3 - 4) \div 2$	$=$	$(6 - 4) \div 2$
	$=$	$2 \div 2$
	$=$	1

Start brackets calculation
Finish brackets calculation
Division last

Exercise 2: Calculate the following:

$3 + 4 \times 6 - 4 \div 2 \quad =$

$3 \times (8 + 2) - 2 + 9 =$

$(5 \times 2 - 2) \div 4 \qquad =$

$6 + 6 \times (5 - 3) - 3 =$

Simple decimals

Decimals are a way of showing that we only have part of a whole. When we write a decimal we write the whole number to the left of the decimal point and the fractional part to the right of the decimal point.

For example: the number 0.34 is less than 1

the number 1.34 is greater than 1

The important rule to remember when adding or subtracting decimals on paper is to always line up the decimal points and numbers in columns.

Example 4:

0.34 + 3.465 + 56.234 + 123.234

```
    0.34
    3.465
   56.234
  123.234
  _____
  183.273
```

Example 5:

456.75 – 34.25

```
   456.75
    34.25
  _____
   422.50
```

Exercise 3: Calculate the following without using a calculator:

1.67 + 2.21   =

5.78 + 3.62   =

3.22 + 10.56   =

15.78 – 5.56   =

21.34 – 6.34   =

450.15 – 10.05   =

There are special rules if you want to multiply or divide decimal numbers by 10.

To multiply by 10, move the decimal point one place to the right. If it is a whole number just add a zero.

Example: 35.45 x 10 = 354.5
            256.7 x 10 = 2,567
            56 x 10 = 560

To multiply by 100, move the decimal point two places to the right, adding zeros if you get to the end. If it is a whole number add two zeros.

Example: 34.5 x 100 = 3,450
            23 x 100 = 2,300

To multiply by 1000, move the decimal point three places to the right, adding zeros if you get to the end. If it is a whole number add three zeros.

Example: 78.23 x 1,000 = 78,230
            12 x 1,000 = 12,000

To divide by 10, move the decimal point one place to the left. Insert leading zeros as necessary.

Example: 35.45 ÷ 10 = 3.545
            89.6 ÷ 10 = 8.96
            0.78 ÷ 10 = 0.078

To divide by 100, move the decimal point two places to the left. Insert leading zeros as necessary.

Example: 675 ÷ 100 = 6.75
            3.2 ÷ 100 = 0.032

To divide by 1000, move the decimal point three places to the left. Insert leading zeros as necessary.

Example: 675 ÷ 1,000 = 0.675
            4.5 ÷ 1,000 = 0.0045

Exercise 4: Calculate the following without using a calculator:
            3,789 x 100   =
            3,654.6 x 1,000 =
            79.345 x 10   =
            156.89 ÷ 100   =
            2.43 ÷ 100   =
            12.785 ÷ 10   =

Simple fractions

When numbers are written as fractions, the whole of something is divided into a number of equal parts. So for example if a chocolate bar bought from the Sports Club vending machine is divided into 5 equal pieces, then each piece equals one fifth of the whole bar.

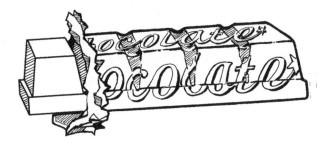

We write this as $^1/_5$.

The number below the line tells us how many equal parts there are – 5 in this case. This is called the **denominator.**

The number above the line tells us how many of these equal parts we are talking about – 1 in this case. This is called the **numerator.**

If we were to take 3 pieces of the chocolate bar we would be taking 3 of the 5 equal parts which is called $^3/_5$ or three fifths.

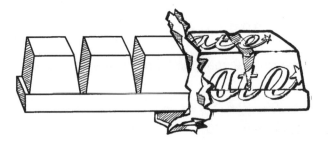

If you need to calculate a fraction of a quantity it can sound quite complicated.

Suppose you are asked "What is $^3/_5$ of 180?" You probably will not be able to work this out in your head. You need to use a paper and pencil, or a calculator, to do it as follows:

Divide the number by the bottom half of the fraction (the denominator) and then multiply by the top half (the numerator) like this.

180 ÷ 5 = 36
36 x 3 = 108
Answer = 108

Example 6:
To find $^7/_8$ of 128:
128 ÷ 8 = 16
16 x 7 = 112
Answer = 112

Exercise 5: What is $^4/_5$ of 180?
What is $^2/_3$ of 711?
What is $^9/_{10}$ of 455?
What is $^3/_7$ of 49?

Percentages

A percentage is a fraction with a denominator of 100. So percent means 'out of a hundred'. 10% means 10 divided by 100.

To work out the answer when it is given as a percentage of a number (e.g. 10% of 150): Answer = percentage ÷ 100 x number

Example 7:

Suppose you were asked to find 56% of 300

Answer = 56 ÷ 100 x 300

= 168

Example 8:

Find 23% of 50

Answer = 23 ÷ 100 x 50

= 11.5

Exercise 6: What is 8% of 400?

What is 45% of 20?

If you are asked to write a number as a percentage of another number:

Answer = (First number ÷ second number) x 100

Tip:

In this case the 'first 'number is generally the smaller one.

Example 9:

What percentage is 168 of 300?

(168 ÷ 300) x 100 = 56%

If you are asked "What percentage of 20 is 18"?

The first step here is to reword this in a way that you are familiar with.

E.g. what percentage is 18 of 20?

(18 ÷ 20) x 100 = 90%

Exercise 7: What percentage is 42 of 600?

What percentage of 125 is 40?

Increasing an amount by a given percentage

If you are told that the annual club membership fee is to be increased by 10% it means that the membership will cost what it was last year plus the 10% increase.

To calculate the new membership fee you must use the method shown above to calculate 10% of last year's fee, and then add it on to last years fee.

Example 10:

Last year the membership fee was £350, and next year it will increase by 10%. What will the membership fee be next year?

The increase = 10% of 350

= 10 ÷ 100 x 350 = £35

The new fee = the old fee + the increase

= 350 + 35

Answer = £385

Exercise 8: You earn £15 for a Saturday job and you have a pay increase of 15%. How much will you earn now?

To decrease an amount by a given percentage

Suppose the club is offering a special deal to attract new members and offers 10% discount on next year's membership.

To calculate the new membership fee you must use the method shown previously to calculate 10% of last year's fee, and then subtract it from last year's fee.

Example 11:

Last year the membership fee was £350, next year it will decrease by 10%. What will the membership fee be next year?

The decrease = 10% of 350

= 10 ÷ 100 x 350 = £35

The new rate = the old fee - the decrease

= 350 - 35

Answer = £315

Exercise 9: A jacket you like was £56, but is discounted by 20% in a sale. How much will it cost now?

Ratios

A ratio is a proportion. For example you will often see instructions that tell you to mix two ingredients together in certain proportions.

In this case 1 part of carpet shampoo to 5 parts water can be written as a ratio 1:5.

It does not matter what is used to measure the carpet shampoo and the water as long as they are both measured with the same container.

e.g. 1 capful of carpet shampoo to 5 capfuls of water or 1 bucketful of carpet shampoo to 5 bucketfuls of water.

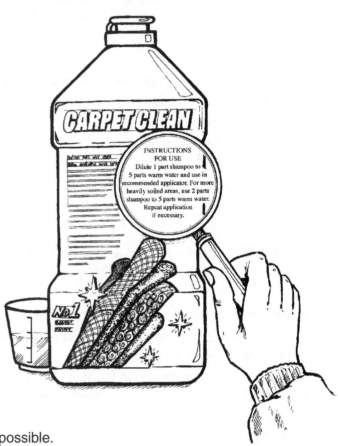

Ratios should be as simple as possible.

You can simplify a ratio by dividing each side by the same number.

Example 12:

Simplify the ratio 100:200

Both numbers can be divided by 100.

So the ratio becomes 1:2 **in its simplest form.**

Tip:

We say that 100 is a **common factor.**

Example 13:

Simplify the ratio 15:21

Both numbers can be divided by 3

So the ratio becomes 5:7

Exercise 10: Write the following ratios in their simplest form:

4:16

6:36

12:60

50:75

Exercise 11: Write the ratios for the following quantities in their simplest form:

22mm, 66mm

40cm, 280cm

9 ml, 12ml

175g, 25g

£12, £40

Proportional values

Sometimes we have a total amount but want to know what the size of each part would be based on a particular ratio.

Example 14:

If there are always 4 times as many boys in a class as there are girls, how many boys will there be in a class of 45?

Ratio is 1 girl to 4 boys i.e. 1:4

First find the total number of parts which make up the whole amount: i.e. 1 + 4 = 5

Find out how much each part represents: Value of each part = 45 ÷ 5 = 9

Find out how many girls and how many boys by multiplying the number of parts by the value of each part:

Girls 1 x 9 = 9

Boys 4 x 9 = 36

Answer   = 36 boys

Example 15:

A sum of money is divided between Alex and Joe in the ratio 2:5. If Alex receives £7, how much does Joe receive?

The total number of parts making up the whole amount is 2 + 5 = 7

Alex has 2 parts = £7

Therefore 1 part = £3.50

Joe has 5 parts = 5 x £3.50 Answer = £17.50

Application of Number **2**

Areas

The **area** of a rectangle is its length multiplied by its width. The units used must be the same for both of the sides.

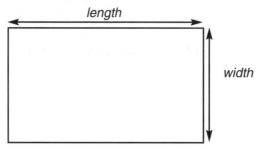

Example 16:

The Sports Club has decided to install a new splash pool for the under Fives. They have received the following price list from the supplier:

Splash pool sizes (length x width)	Splash pool prices
1m x 2m	£1,100
3m x 2m	£1,900
4m x 2m	£2,300
4m x 3m	£3,000

The club need to calculate how much floor area this new pool will take.

If they choose the 3m x 2m pool, the area will be:

Area   = length x width

$\quad$ = 3 x 2 m^2

$\quad$ = 6 m^2 (pronounced 6 square metres)

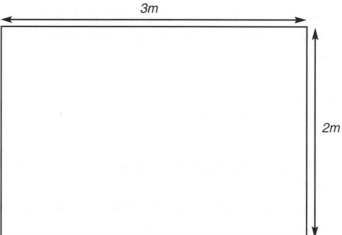

Exercise 12: What is the area of the largest splash pool on the price list?

Volumes

The club also needs to know the amount of space the new pool will occupy when it is dug into the ground, so that they can calculate how much water it will take to fill it. They need to find out the **volume** of the splash pool in cubic metres.

If you imagine the splash pool as a solid shape, it would be called a **cuboid.**

To calculate the volume we need to know three dimensions: the length, width and height.

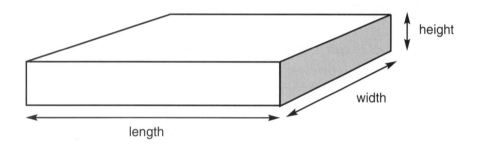

Volume = length x width x height

Example 17:

All the splash pools on the supplier's price list are half a metre deep.

So the volume of the 3m x 2m pool will be:

Volume   = length x width x height

               = 3 x 2 x 0.5 m^3

               = 3 m^3 (pronounced three cubic metres)

Exercise 13: What is the volume of the smallest splash pool?

Exercise 14: What is the volume of the largest splash pool?

Tip:
All the units must be the same

Chapter 8
Calculations

Application of Number **2**

Using straightforward scales on diagrams

If we wanted to draw a picture of one of the proposed splash pools it would obviously have to be smaller than the actual pool otherwise we wouldn't have a piece of paper big enough! But the reduction in size needs be in a fixed proportion to the real pool measurements. This is called the scale of a drawing. You will probably have seen scales used on maps too.

Example 18:

On a road map, if the scale is 1:500,000 this means that 1cm on the map is 500,000cm of road (5000m).

Example 19:

The largest splash pool drawn to a scale of 1:100, would look like this:

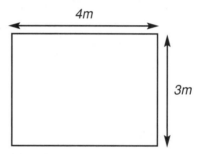

4m

3m

Check this with your ruler. 1cm on the diagram equals 100cm (1m) of the pool.

Exercise 15: Draw a scale diagram of the 3m x 2m splash pool.

Exercise 16: Below is part of the map from the Broomhill brochure showing its location. The scale is 1:6,000. Use your ruler to estimate the length of Manley St, from the traffic lights on High Street to Majors Corner roundabout.

Finding an average

You may be asked to find the average of a list of numbers.

There are different types of average.

Mean

The **mean** is the most common type of average.

To calculate the mean, you add up all the numbers and then divide by the number of items.

Example 20:

The club has received complaints about the temperature of the water in the swimming pool. You have been asked to calculate the mean (average) temperature of the swimming pool over a period of two hours. You decide to take the readings every fifteen minutes. These are the numbers (or **data**) that you produce.

Time	Temperature (°C)
10.00	28
10.15	29
10.30	27
10.45	26
11.00	28
11.15	25
11.30	25
11.45	28
12.00	27

To calculate the mean temperature over the two hours:

Mean $= \dfrac{28 + 29 + 27 + 26 + 28 + 25 + 25 + 28 + 27}{9}$

$= \dfrac{243}{9} = 27°\,C$

The temperature should be an average 28°C, so perhaps the staff need to turn up the heating a little!

Exercise 17: If only the first four readings had been taken what would the average temperature be?

Exercise 18: The temperature in the sauna was measured once a day for 7 days. The readings were as follows:

35, 32, 31, 31, 31, 36, 35

What was the average temperature over the seven days?

Median

To find the median you need to arrange the data in order from smallest to largest and then select the middle number. If there is an even number of items then find the mean of the two middle items.

Example 21:

To find the median temperature in the table on the previous page.
Rearrange the numbers in order:

25 25 26 27 27 28 28 28 29

Find the middle number

The median temperature over the two hours is 27°C

Exercise 19: Calculate the median number of students attending an evening class. The numbers attending were:

14, 12, 13, 11, 13, 15, 10

Exercise 20: Calculate the median weight of these cakes:

2.5kg, 2kg, 2kg, 2.4kg, 2.1kg, 2.6kg, 2kg

Mode

To find the mode, you have to find which value occurs most often. If you look at the list of temperatures in the table on the previous page you can see that the temperature 28°C occurs most often – so this is the mode.

Exercise 21: Calculate the modal number of students attending an evening class each week. The numbers attending were:

14, 12, 13, 11, 13, 15,10

Exercise 22: Calculate the modal shoe size of seven schoolchildren:

6, 7, 6, 8, 9, 6, 5

Find a range

The range of a series of numbers is the gap between the largest and the smallest. To find the range, find the highest and the lowest numbers and subtract them.

Example 22:

To find the range of temperatures in the table on the previous page:

Highest number = 29

Lowest number   = 25

Range = 29 – 25 = 4°C

Exercise 23: Find the range of attendances at an evening class over a period of 7 weeks:

14, 12, 13, 11, 13, 15,10

Exercise 24: Find the range of the number of matches in 7 boxes:

29, 31, 28, 29, 30, 30, 29

Approximation

Sometimes it is OK to give an approximate figure. If we say that the population of the UK is 60 million we do not mean exactly that number – a completely accurate figure would be impossible. In this case the number has been rounded to the nearest million.

Example 23:

To round a number to the nearest 10, the number is written as the nearest multiple of 10.

138 would be rounded up to 140 and 112 would be rounded down to 110.

Example 24:

To round a number to the nearest 100, the number is written as the nearest multiple of 100.

1,678 would be rounded up to 1,700 and 1,229 would be rounded down to 1,200.

Sometimes decimal numbers are rounded to a certain number of decimal places.

Example 25:

To round the number 25.638 to 2 decimal places we need to look at the third digit after the decimal point. If this digit is 5 or more then round up, if this digit is 4 or less, then round down.

In this case the third digit after the decimal point is 8, so we round up and the number becomes 25.64.

Exercise 25: Round 3,678,899 to the nearest thousand.

Exercise 26: Round 3.4556 to 2 decimal places.

Exercise 27: Round 67.23 to 1 decimal place.

Tip:

When you multiply 10 by any other number, the answer you get will be a multiple of 10.

Chapter 8
Calculations

Application of Number **2**

Checking calculations

In earlier sections you have been carrying out different types of calculation. You should always check the results of your calculations to be sure they make sense. Here are a few techniques that you can use.

Estimation

When performing calculations, either by calculator, in your head or on paper, it is a good idea to estimate the final value to check the answer.

Example 26:

Estimate the value of 19.63 x 31.23

19.63 is approximately 20

31.23 is approximately 30

The estimated answer is 20 x 30 = 600

Exercise 28: Some of these calculations are wrong. Find by estimation which are correct and which ones are wrong.

$$29 \times 49 = 1,421$$
$$0.53 \times 241 = 1,277.3$$
$$197 \div 3.94 = 75$$
$$27.58 \div 5.1 = 5.4$$

Inverse operations

This means checking your calculations by working backwards from your answer.

Example 27:

Use your calculator to work out 6,756 + 8,222

Subtract 6,756 from your answer. You should get 8,222.

Work out 6,756 + 8,222 again.

This time subtract 8,222 from your answer. You should get 6,756.

Example 28:

Use your calculator to work out 25 x 32

Divide your answer by 25. You should get 32.

Work out 25 x 32 again.

This time divide your answer by 32. You should get 25.

Exercise 29: Work out on your calculator 125 − 89

What would you expect to get if you added 89 to your answer?

Exercise 30: Work out on your calculator 330 ÷ 15

What would you expect to get if you multiplied your answer by 15?

Sample Assignment

Background

You are asked to help the manager of Novus supermarket by performing some calculations on the data supplied in the previous assignment (Chapter 7). Be sure to show all of your working and any checks that you have performed on your calculations.

Tasks

1   Calculate what percentage of the total staff work in the chilled, superchilled and frozen areas combined. To how many decimal places should you answer and why?

2   Complete the following table:

Section(s)	Area (m^2)	% of total area	Fraction of total area
Vegetables PLUS Fruit			
Dairy PLUS Frozen			
Canned foods			

3   What is the ratio of staff working in the Fruit and Vegetables sections to those working in the superchilled and frozen areas combined?

4   What is the ratio of male employees to female employees?

5   If the total wage bill for the people shown in the table is £3,000 per week and everyone earns the same amount, how much is the combined wage bill per week for the men?

6   If a pay rise of 5% was awarded, how much would each female receive per week?

7   If employees work 37.5 hours per week, how much per hour would they earn after the pay rise?

8   What is the average (mean) value per section of sales per week in thousands of pounds? Give your answer to 1 decimal place.

9   What is the modal area of a section?

10 In the column headed **Approx. sales values per week** what does 28.3 represent expressed as a whole figure?

11 Find the range of the average number of items stocked in the sections.

12 A container for potatoes has the following dimensions: height 120cm, length 80cm, width 50cm. What is the volume of the container?

13 The total floor space allocated to potatoes is 2.4m long and 0.5m wide. How many containers can they display?

14 What area of floor (in m^2) would they occupy?

Evidence to collect

•   Answers to tasks 1 – 14, neatly presented and showing your working.

•   Notes of checks that you have performed on the calculations.

Chapter 8
Calculations

Relating the assignment to the specification

Specification Reference (Part B)	What has been done to satisfy this
N1.1	
• Obtain the information you need to meet the purpose of your task.	
• Identify suitable calculations to get the results you need.	
N1.2	
• Carry out calculations to the levels of accuracy you have been given.	• Tasks 1-14
• Check your results make sense.	• Tasks 1-14
N1.3	
• Choose suitable ways to present your findings.	
• Present your findings clearly.	
• Describe how the results of your calculations meet the purposes of your task	

Other Key Skills signposting

Information Technology IT1.1

Ideas for other assignments

❗ Calculations based on the results of science experiments.

❗ Calculations based on the analysis of newspaper reports on, for example, crime rates, population growth, global warming etc.

❗ Calculations based on the analysis of company performance found in a company's Annual Report.

❗ Calculations based around a budget for a holiday or household expenses.

❗ Calculations of business expenses.

Sample test questions

Use the information below for questions 1 and 2.

Jenny is planning to renew the floor covering of her kitchen. The floor is 3.85m wide and 4.78m long.

1 She uses a calculator to find the area of the floor. She wants to check that her calculated answer is about right. Which of these quick checks should she use?

A 3 x 5

B 4 x 5

C 3 x 6

D 4 x 6

2 She plans to cover the floor with vinyl tiles. Each tile is 0.5m by 0.5m. How many tiles will she need?

A 96

B 48

C 60

D 80

3 A group of local workers won the lottery – six people shared £1,800,036. How much did each of the six workers get?

A £30,006

B £300,006

C £3 000,006

D £360,000

4 Dom and Sharif spent £8 between them on their lottery tickets one week. Dom put in £3 and Sharif put in £5. They have agreed to share the winnings according to the amount they put in. To their amazed delight, they win £64,000. How much will each get?

A Dom will get £16,000 and Sharif will get £48,000

B Dom will get £48,000 and Sharif will get £16,000

C Dom will get £24,000 and Sharif will get £40,000

D Dom will get £40,000 and Sharif will get £24,000

Use the information below for questions 5, 6 and 7.

Katie works in a supermarket. She is paid £5.25 per hour.

5   Katie needs to earn at least £165 a week. How should she calculate the
    number of hours she has to work each week?

    A   165 ÷ 5.25

    B   5.25 ÷ 165

    C   5.25 x 165

    D   165 - 5.25

6   Last week Katie worked 38 hours. This was 10 hours more than she
    normally works. How much more did she earn last week, compared with a
    normal week?

    A   £52.50

    B   £104.50

    C   £5.25

    D   £22.007

7   Katie is paid for each complete quarter hour she works. She works
    5 hours 10 minutes on one day. How long will she be paid for?

    A $5^1/_4$ hours

    B $5^1/_2$ hours

    C   5 hours

    D   6 hours

Use the information below for questions 8, 9 and 10.

Mr and Mrs Garcia decide to create a patio in their garden.

8   They estimate that the space to be paved is about 2.5 metres by 5.2 metres.
    Using these values, what is the area of the patio?

    A $10m^2$

    B $13m^2$

    C $16m^2$

    D $2.5m^2$

9   When Mr Garcia measures more accurately, he finds that the actual area is
    $14.94m^2$. Round this result to the nearest 0.5 square metres.

    A $14.8m^2$

    B $14m^2$

    C $15m^2$

    D $14.9m^2$

10 The paving stones are each $1m^2$ and come in packs of 6. How many
    packs will Mr Garcia need to create his patio?

    A   3

    B   6

    C   14

    D   2

Use the information below for questions 11 and 12.

Alisha has been babysitting for several neighbours. Over the past 10 weeks she has earned the following amounts:

£15 £12 £15 £18 £18 £20 £12 £18 £20 £12

11   What is the mean amount she has earned?

   A   £18
   B   £16
   C   £12
   D   £20

12   What is the range of Alisha's earnings?

   A   £20
   B   £12
   C   £8
   D   £5

13   A surveyor makes scale drawings for different parts of a new building. On the scale drawing, the width of a room measures 5.7 centimetres. The scale of the drawing is 10mm to 1m. The actual width of the room is:

   A   5.7m
   B   50.7m
   C   57m
   D   0.57m

14   If there are 5 times as many male employees in a company as there are females, how many males will there be if the total number of employees is 360?

   A   60
   B   30
   C   36
   D   300

15   A computer game, originally costing £35, has been reduced by 20% in a sale. How much will it cost now?

   A   £15
   B   £28
   C   £25
   D   £30

16   A cake tin is 22cm long by 12.5cm wide by 6.5cm deep. What is the volume of cake that would fill the tin?

   A $1787.5cm^2$
   B $41cm^2$
   C $1787.5cm^3$
   D $41cm^3$

Chapter 9
Presenting Results

In Chapter 7 you were gathering and interpreting data from different sources. In Chapter 8 you moved on to perform calculations on data. The final stage is to present your findings clearly.

There are different ways to present your findings. You may choose to present the results of an observation exercise in a pictogram or a frequency diagram. Alternatively you may decide that a bar chart, pie chart or line graph is more appropriate.

Whichever form of presentation you decide to use, be sure to label your work. Always add a title to a chart or diagram. Label the axes of a chart and make sure that the scale shows your results clearly.

Once you feel everything is clear, write a brief explanation of how the results meet your original purpose.

Types of chart

The easiest way to present a table of information and then convert it into a chart is to use a spreadsheet package on the computer. You will have to do this for your IT Key Skills and so you may be able to use the same evidence for both. You will find instructions on how to create tables and charts using Microsoft Excel in Chapter 5 of this book.

However it is up to you to decide which type of chart to use. In Chapter 7 we looked at the most common types of graph and chart – here is a summary.

Type of chart/graph	Description
Pictogram	This uses symbols to show how many units of data belong in a group.
Bar chart	This is one of the most common ways of showing information. It uses the length of a bar against a scale to show how many units of data belong in a group. The bars are normally shown vertically but they can also be shown horizontally.
Pie chart	This is a circular diagram where each group is shown as a proportion of the whole amount, and is represented by a sector of the circle.
Line graph	This shows how information changes between consecutive values or over a period of time.

Presenting your results

Having chosen which type of chart to produce you must be sure to present it clearly.

! The chart should have a main title that describes what the chart shows.

! The X and Y axes should be clearly labelled.

! Regular points along the X and Y axes should be labelled, making it easy to read off values.

! The accuracy of the chart will be limited by the size of its scale. Generally you should always use the largest scale that will fit in the space available.

! If you are producing a line graph or bar chart, think about displaying horizontal and vertical gridlines to make it easier to read off values.

! Use different colours in graphs and charts if you are showing more than one set of data. If your work is not going to be printed in colour, then think about using different patterns for different sectors of pie charts.

If you are presenting the results of calculations always show the method you have used – you may get some credit even if you made a slip in the final answer. Always show the units of measurement that you are using and make sure you follow instructions to display answers to certain numbers of decimal places.

If you have performed calculations or drawn charts to find the answer to a specific question, remember to conclude at the end with the answer to that original question. This shows how your calculations relate to the purpose of the task.

Sample Assignment

Background

The manager of Novus is preparing a report and a presentation for the directors at Head Office. He asks you to prepare some diagrams and charts for him to use.

Tasks

The manager wants to know what kind of people shop in his store so he asked a student on work experience to observe people entering the store. This is an extract from her records.

Male adult	Female child	Female adult	Female adult
Female adult	Female adult	Female senior citizen	Male adult
Male teenager	Male senior citizen	Male adult	Male teenager
Female senior citizen	Male child	Female adult	Female adult
Male senior citizen	Male adult	Male teenager	Female adult
Female adult	Female adult	Female senior citizen	Male adult
Male teenager	Male senior citizen	Male adult	Female adult
Female child	Female senior citizen	Male adult	Male teenager
Female adult	Female adult	Female adult	Female senior citizen

1   Prepare a tally chart from this data.

2   Draw a bar chart from this data. Give the chart a title and label the axes.

3   In the past the manager has not stocked food in small portions (i.e. suitable for senior citizens) because he assumed the majority of his custom was from families. Calculate the percentage of senior citizens in this sample. Was the manager correct in his assumption?

4   Refer back to the table of data provided by the manager for the assignment at the end of Chapter 7. Represent the floor space for the different areas (i.e. chilled, frozen etc.) in a pie chart. Which column of data will you use and why?

5   Five boxes of fruit are stacked on a shelf next to each other. They are all the same width (50cm) but their lengths vary as follows: apples 110cm, pears 70cm, oranges 120cm, bananas 140cm, grapes 40cm. Draw a scale diagram of the boxes on the shelf. Remember to state what scale you have used.

Evidence to collect

- Answers to tasks 1 – 5, neatly presented. You can use a computer to produce the charts and diagrams if you wish.

Relating the assignment to the specification

Specification Reference (Part B)	What has been done to satisfy this
N1.1	
• Obtain the information you need to meet the purpose of your task.	
• Identify suitable calculations to get the results you need.	
N1.2	
• Carry out calculations to the levels of accuracy you have been given.	
• Check your results make sense.	
N1.3	
• Choose suitable ways to present your findings.	• Tasks 1-5
• Present your findings clearly.	• Tasks 1-5
• Describe how the results of your calculations meet the purposes of your task	• Tasks 1-5

Other Key Skills signposting
Information Technology IT1.2
Communication C1.3

Ideas for other assignments
Charts of results from science experiments.

Charts showing the results of calculations based on newspaper reports on crime rates, population growth, global warming etc.

Charts showing different areas of company performance.

Sample test questions

1   Christian wants to use a chart to show how many hours in an average day he spends doing certain things. Which of these four charts shows this most clearly?

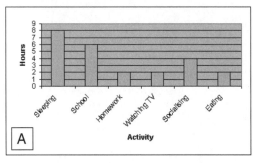

A

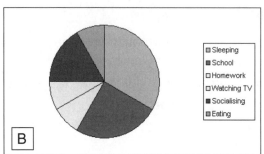

B

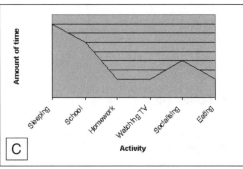

C

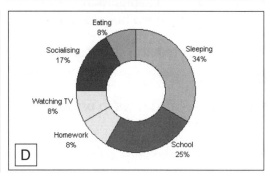

D

A   A
B   B
C   C
D   D

2   This chart compares the results of the students in a school, in English and Mathematics exams. What is wrong with the chart?

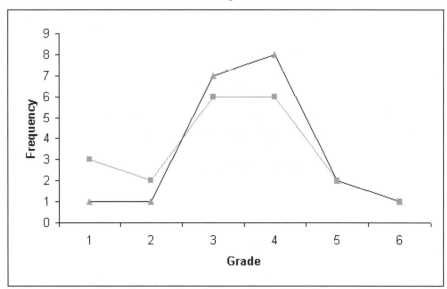

    A   the axes are not labelled

    B   the scale is wrong

    C   there is no legend

    D   the lines are too long

3   Susie hands in the following calculation to her teacher.

Volume of a cube which has sides of length 4cm = 64

What is wrong with her answer?

    A   the answer should be 12

    B   the answer should be $64cm^3$

    C   the answer should be 64cm

    D   the answer should be 24

4   What is wrong with this pie chart showing how a family spend their weekly wage?

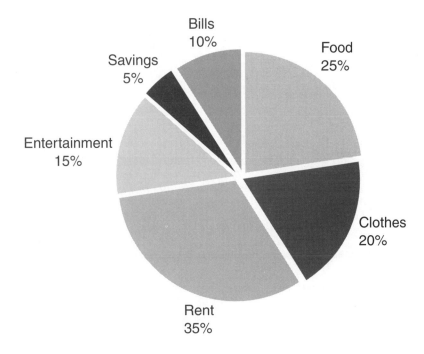

    A   the categories are wrong

    B   they do not save enough

    C   their rent is too high

    D   the percentages are wrong

Part 3

Communication (3)

Chapter 10
Taking Part in Discussions

One-to-one discussions

A one-to-one discussion involves only two people. The conversation should be a two-way process, with a clear exchange of information between the two people.

The conversation could be face-to face – here are some examples:

! Stopping someone in the street and asking them directions.

! Being stopped by someone in a shop and asked the time.

! Being interviewed for a job.

! Discussing your homework with a teacher.

! Chatting with your mother about what to have for dinner.

Sometimes you will know the person and sometimes you will not. The person you are speaking to, and the situation in which the conversation takes place, both influence how you speak.

Generally you need to take extra care in the following situations:

! When you are speaking to someone of a different status.

! When you are speaking to someone you have not met before.

In these situations you need to pay particular attention to:

! The kind of words you choose.

! The tone of voice you use.

! The message you want to get across to the other person.

Interviews

One of the most important one-to-one, face-to-face discussions you are likely to have is a job interview. Although you may feel that this is a case of you answering all of the questions, it really shouldn't be. It should still be a two-way process, giving you the opportunity to find out about the company as well as them finding out about you. Here are some useful tips:

- ! Use appropriate body language and facial expressions (e.g. head nodding shows interest, foot tapping shows impatience).

- ! Have some notes with you to remind you of the important points you want to make and questions you want to ask.

- ! Give yourself time to think about your answers and not to say the first thing that comes into your head.

- ! If you are told some important information be prepared to note it down.

- ! Check you have understood certain points by repeating them back.

- ! Use appropriate tones of voice.

- ! Make eye-contact with the person who is interviewing you.

Tip:
A good rule to remember is that you should listen twice as much as you talk.

Exercise 1: Which of these interviewees do you think is most confident and why?

Tip:
If you see +44 at the beginning of a UK telephone number don't be confused – this is simply the International code for people phoning from overseas.

Talking on the telephone

Telephone calls can take two forms:

! The ones you make yourself, and

! The ones you receive

Before you make a business telephone call there are four things to ask yourself:

! With whom do you want to speak?

! What are you going to say to them?

! What result do you want from the conversation?

! When is the best time of day to make the call?

So, make sure you have the person's exact name or you may be passed from department to department. Jot down some notes of what you are going to say and be clear about what result you want before ending the call. Think about the time of day – if someone finishes work at 5.00pm, they may not appreciate a call from you at 4.58pm.

Remember that the way you treat someone who telephones you leaves the caller with an impression of you and possibly of the organisation for which you work.

When answering a telephone call:

! Be polite and friendly and sound interested.

! Give the caller your full attention.

! Make notes of any message you have to pass on to someone else.

! Give the caller the choice of holding or getting back to them.

! Speak slowly and clearly.

! Don't leave people waiting on the line for more than a minute.

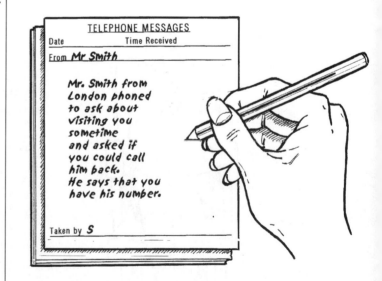

Exercise 2: What is wrong with this message?

Group discussions

Holding a class debate is a good way of involving a group of people in a discussion. If this is taped it can be used as part of your key skills evidence.

A debate is organised in the following way.

! A subject is chosen. This should be something that the majority of the class are interested in and hold a view on.

! A statement to be debated should be identified. (This is called the **motion**.)

! The class should be divided into two groups. One group will be arguing in favour of the motion (the 'ayes') and the second group will be arguing against the motion (the 'noes').

! The teacher, or other nominated person (the proposer), should write the motion on the board and read it aloud.

! The 'ayes' take it in turns to state one argument in favour of the motion.

! The 'noes' then take it in turns to state one argument against.

! The 'ayes' then have the opportunity to rebut the arguments from the opposing side.

! The 'noes' then have the opportunity to rebut the arguments from the opposition.

! Open discussion is then allowed for a fixed period of time. The proposer takes a final vote and declares the motion either carried or not.

Here are some tips for group discussions:

! Be aware of other group members.

! Be polite.

! Wait for people to finish speaking.

! Speak clearly.

! Don't lose your temper.

! Don't dominate the discussion.

! Don't be silent.

Chapter 10
Taking Part in Discussions

Communication 3

Listening

A good listener pays attention to the person speaking and takes an interest in what they've got to say. It is easy to tell when someone is hearing your voice but not actually listening to what you are saying – their eyes glaze over and they may even stifle a yawn!

You can use different techniques to let people know you are listening. You can offer an occasional nod or word of approval like "OK" or "mmm". You can ask a question about what the other person has been saying, or ask them to clarify a point.

Exercise 3: Can you think of any other ways of letting people know you are listening to what they are saying?

Sample Assignment

Background

Work in groups of between 4 and 6 people.

You are asked to undertake some research into television 'soaps'. Why are they so popular? Who watches them most? Which are the most popular? The group will prepare a survey and each group member will interview at least one person using the prepared questions.

Tasks

1   Organise four meetings:

  • One to elect an initial chairperson, someone to take the minutes and someone to prepare the agendas for future meetings. These roles should be rotated amongst group members over the following meetings.

  • One to prepare the survey questions.

  • One to report progress.

  • One to report back findings.

2   Tape at least one of the meetings to record each member's contribution to the group discussion.

3   During the group meetings, all group members should:

  • Contribute relevant and appropriate comments.

  • Be prepared to listen to other people.

  • Not dominate the conversation.

4   Each group member must then interview one person on a one-to-one basis. During the interview you must:

  • Make sure that the interviewee is clear about the purpose of the interview and what you are trying to get out of the discussion.

  • Explain the questions.

  • Listen carefully to the answers.

  • Note the answers down.

  • Follow up on any questions to clarify any points if necessary.

Evidence to be collected

- Notes from at least one of the meetings explaining what your role was, together with any document you produced for the meeting e.g. agenda, minutes etc.

- A tape recording of one of the group meetings in which you made a contribution.

- A written statement from your tutor who witnessed your contributions to group meetings.

- Notes of the one-to-one interview that you conducted.

Relating the assignment to the specification

Specification Reference (Part B)	What has been done to satisfy this
C1.1	
• Provide information that is relevant to the subject and purpose of the discussion.	• Tasks 1 – 4
• Speak clearly in a way that suits the situation.	• Tasks 1 – 4
• Listen and respond appropriately to what others say.	• Tasks 1 – 4
C1.2	
• Read the relevant material.	
• Identify accurately the main points and ideas in material.	
• Use the information to suit your purpose.	
C1.3	
• Present relevant information in a form that suits your purpose.	
• Ensure text is legible.	
• Make sure that spelling, punctuation and grammar are accurate so your meaning is clear.	

Ideas for other assignments

❗ A class debate about a current news topic.

❗ A series of interviews conducted as part of a survey to find out people's views on a current news topic.

❗ A presentation to your class on some research you have undertaken, together with a one-to-one interview with your tutor about your work.

Sample test questions

1 You are in an unfamiliar building and you ask a man in a dark suit for directions to a particular office. Which of these would be the best way to speak to him?

A Hey mate, tell us how to get to room E42 will you?

B Excuse me, please could you direct me to room E42?

C Where's room E42?

D I'm lost, where am I?

2 If you were a manager and wanted to ask a work-experience student to do some urgent photocopying, which would be the best way to address him?

A Get this photocopying done, quick!

B Now Dave, be a good little lad and photocopy these for me.

C I would be eternally grateful if you could spare the time to photocopy these for me.

D Dave, please could you photocopy these for me, I need them in half an hour.

3 In the following sentences the stress has been highlighted. Which sentence means that you are being emphatically prohibited from wearing the outfit by someone in authority?

A **You're** not going to wear that outfit.

B You're **not** going to wear that outfit.

C You're not going to **wear** that outfit.

D You're not going to wear **that** outfit.

4 Which of these statements is not factual?

A I think the red jacket is best.

B The red jacket has three pockets.

C The red jacket is more expensive than the black one.

D The black jacket is available in bigger sizes.

5 Which of these body movements would suggest that you are not listening intently to a speaker?

A Yawning

B Nodding your head

C Looking puzzled

D Shaking your head

6   Which of these is not a good telephone manner?

A   Being polite

B   Being helpful

C   Speaking quickly

D   Being friendly

7   When talking to a group of people you should:

A   speak as quietly as possible

B   stare out of the window

C   speak slowly and clearly

D   face the other way

8   Which of these is the best way to answer a telephone call?

A   Good Morning, Brains Publishers, Jane speaking, how can I help you?

B   Hi, Jane here, can I help?

C   Yes?

D   Hello, Brains, how can I help?

9   If you were telephoning your local MP's office, how would you ask for her?

A   Hi, can I speak to Geraldine?

B   Hello, please could you put me through to Geraldine Harper?

C   Geraldine Harper

D   I want to speak to Miss Harper

10   In a group meeting you should never:

A   speak

B   make notes

C   listen to others

D   interrupt other people speaking

Chapter 11
Reading and Obtaining Information

You will often have to find out or look up information. Reasons for needing information can include:

! Research for a work or school/college-related activity.

! Social activities: e.g. what's on at the local cinema.

! How to use something you have just bought: e.g. DVD player.

! General interest: e.g. where Manchester United are in the League tables.

Exercise 1: Think over what you did yesterday and what information you looked for and why.

Main sources of written information

Much of the information that you look for will be written down in text format. Some of these sources include:

! Books

! Newspapers

! Magazines

! Newsletters

! Web sites

! CD-ROMs

! Teletext

! Instruction manuals

! Publicity material e.g. posters, leaflets, adverts

You need to know where to find certain types of information and be able to say which is the quickest, most convenient or cheapest source.

Example 1:

If I wanted to find out what the temperature was in Paris yesterday, the easiest and quickest source would probably be a national newspaper or a web site such as the BBC Weather site *(www.bbc.co.uk/weather)*. No book (or magazine) would give me such recent information. Teletext might tell me what the temperature is today and what it will be for the next few days, but not what it was yesterday.

Example 2:

If I bought a new car and I needed to find out what the tyre pressures should be I would look it up in the manual supplied with the car. This would probably be the only written source, unless a car manual has been published in book form for my particular car – however this would involve me in a trip to the library or book shop.

Exercise 2: There are lots of text-based sources to tell you what will be on the television this evening. How many can you think of?

Getting advice and help from other people

Sometimes you cannot access the information directly yourself – you need to ask someone else. You may ask for facts or you may ask someone for ideas or their opinion about something. Think about who you could ask for information and the type of information they are likely to give you. They may include the following:

- Peers – facts, instructions, opinions, ideas

- Tutors/supervisors – facts, instructions, opinions, ideas

- Parents/relatives – facts, instructions, opinions, ideas

- Libraries – facts, instructions

- Other organisations (e.g. companies, charities, Tourist Information Centres, museums etc.) – facts

There are different ways of asking for information:

- A face-to-face visit

- Telephone

- Writing a letter

Exercise 3: Look at the list of people above. For each of them decide if it would be most appropriate to ask them for information face-to-face, via a telephone call or with a letter.

Working out the main points

Sometimes you read text from the beginning to the end – for example if you were reading a story. If you just want to find out some information quickly there are some different methods of reading that you might find useful:

Skim-reading is to read quite quickly, just to get a rough idea what the information is about. If you have skim-read something you will be able to give a brief outline of the piece of writing, but will not be able to give many details.

Scan-reading is when you search through a piece of writing for an item of information. You ignore anything that is not important to you and concentrate on finding exactly the information you are looking for.

You may combine these two techniques, skimming first to get the main idea and then scanning for particular information.

Exercise 4: Skim the information shown in the brochure at the beginning of this book and summarise the facilities of the club in twenty words.

Then scan the information and answer the following questions:

• How much do aerobics lessons cost per hour?

• What is the name of the club manager?

Relating images to text

Using images can help people understand information and explanations. Sometimes a labelled diagram is needed.

Exercise 5: Read the following:

Directions to Broomhill Sports Club

Travelling from Chelmsford follow the A990 (which becomes High Street as you enter East Harling). At the traffic lights turn left into Manley Road. At the next roundabout take the second exit and Broomhill Sports Club is found on the right-hand side around the bend. Parking is available further up Hale Road.

If you are approaching from Brentwood on the B123, you will pass the Crown Public House on your left. At the next roundabout, take the first exit into Hale Road. Broomhill Sports Club is found on the right-hand side around the bend. Parking is available further up Hale Road.

Exercise 6: Do you agree that looking at a map might be easier?

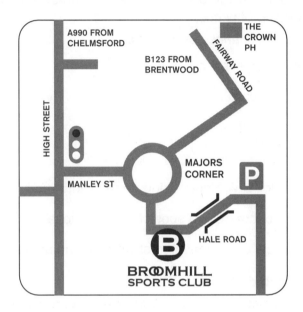

Sometimes no words at all are required if you have a good image!

Exercise 7: Discuss what is happening in this cartoon.

Using a dictionary

Always keep a dictionary handy. It can be used to find the meaning of unfamiliar words and to check the spelling of words.

There are different types of dictionaries, for example:

- Dictionaries for adult native-speakers of English
- Dictionaries for young children
- Dictionaries for different languages
- Picture dictionaries
- Specialist dictionaries (for Law, Engineering, Architecture etc)
- Dictionaries in electronic form (e.g. a spell-checker dictionary)
- Glossaries, which are lists of the meaning of words found at the end of books

How to use an ordinary adult dictionary

Dictionary entries in a normal dictionary for adult native-speakers of English, such as the Concise Oxford English Dictionary, give you different types of information.

If you know how to spell the word but want to know its meaning, then search for the word in the dictionary. It is organised in alphabetical order of the first letter of a word, followed by the second letter in alphabetical order, followed by the third and so on.

The word *digestion* comes before the word digestive in the dictionary because each letter is the same until you reach the letter *o* in *digestion* and the letter *v* in *digestive* - *o* comes before *v* in the alphabet so digestion is listed first.

> **digestion** ● n. the process of digesting. ➤ a person's capacity to digest food.
>
> **digestive** ● adj. of or relating to the process of digesting food. ➤ (of food or medicine) aiding or promoting the process of digestion. ● n. 1 a food or medicine that aids or promotes the digestion of food. 2 Brit. a round semi-sweet biscuit made of wholemeal flour.
> -- DERIVATIVES **digestively** adv.
> -- ORIGIN ME: from OFr. *digestif*, *-ive* or L. *digestivus*, from *digest-*, *digerere* (see **DIGEST**).
>
> **digger** ● n. 1 a person, animal, or large machine that digs earth. 2 (**Digger**) a member of a group of radical dissenters formed as an offshoot of the Levellers, believing

Exercise 8: Put these words into alphabetical order, as they would appear in a dictionary:

Medallion, medal, medallist

If you are not sure of the spelling of a word, then guess the first letter, go to that section in the dictionary, guess the second letter etc.

Using a thesaurus

Not a Jurassic reptile, a thesaurus is the opposite of a dictionary – in this case you know the meaning you want but you can't think of the word. A thesaurus can be very handy when you are doing a crossword.

digestion	166	**dimension**

abridgment, abstract, compendium, con~ densation, epitome, précis, résumé, sum~ mary, synopsis

digestion absorption, assimilation, con~ version, incorporation, ingestion, trans~ formation

dig in 1. defend, entrench, establish, forti~ fy, maintain **2.** *Inf.* begin, set about, start eating, tuck in (*Inf.*)

dignified august, decorous, distinguished, exalted, formal, grave, honourable, im~ posing, lofty, lordly, noble, reserved, sol~ emn, stately, upright

Antonyms unseemly, crass, inelegant, unbecoming, undignified, vulgar

dignify adorn, advance, aggrandize, dis~ tinguish, elevate, ennoble, exalt, glorify, grace, honour, promote, raise

dignitary *n.* bigwig (*Inf.*), celeb (*Inf.*), high-up (*Inf.*), notability, notable, person~ age, pillar of society (the church, the state), public figure, V.I.P., worthy

dignity 1. courtliness, decorum, grandeur, gravity, hauteur, loftiness, majesty, nobil~ ity, propriety, solemnity, stateliness **2.** elevation, eminence, excellence, glory, greatness, honour, importance, nobleness,

Antonyms on-the-ball (*Inf.*), prompt, punctual, sharp (*Inf.*)

dilemma 1. difficulty, embarrassment, fix (*Inf.*), jam (*Inf.*), mess, perplexity, pickle (*Inf.*), plight, predicament, problem, puz~ zle, quandary, spot (*Inf.*), strait, tight cor~ ner *or* spot **2. on the horns of a dilemma** between Scylla and Charybdis, between the devil and the deep blue sea

dilettante aesthete, amateur, dabbler, nonprofessional, trifler

diligence activity, application, assiduity, assiduousness, attention, attentiveness, care, constancy, earnestness, heedfulness, industry, intentness, laboriousness, per~ severance, sedulousness

diligent active, assiduous, attentive, busy, careful, conscientious, constant, earnest, hard-working, indefatigable, industrious, laborious, painstaking, persevering, per~ sistent, sedulous, studious, tireless

Antonyms careless, dilatory, inconstant, indifferent, lazy

dilly-dally dally, dawdle, delay, dither, falter, fluctuate, hesitate, hover, linger, loiter, potter, procrastinate, shillyshally (*Inf.*), trifle, vacillate, waver

Getting information ready to use

Taking notes

If someone is explaining something to you, or if you are reading a piece of writing, you may be asked to make notes.

Your notes should be as brief as possible but they must make sense when you look at them later!

Here are some tips on taking notes:

(!) Don't try to write word for word what the speaker is saying or copy every sentence in a written piece of work.

(!) Read through a written piece of work completely before you start making notes.

(!) Try to develop your own shorthand, using abbreviations where possible, e.g. **info** for information.

(!) Include the main points such as names, dates, events, decisions, reasons etc.

(!) Make your notes short, neat and to the point.

(!) Go through your notes when you have more time and rewrite them if necessary – if you leave them too long you might not understand them when you need them.

There are two main ways of taking notes that you may find useful:

> Linear notes
>
> Web notes or patterned notes

Linear notes are the usual kind of notes people make. The word linear means in a straight line and that is how linear notes are written – in a straight line across the page. Linear also means or implies, from beginning to end, i.e. you make notes in the order that points arise, each point following the one before on the page. You list the main points under headings and subheadings.

Web notes or patterned notes look more like a picture or a plan, with even fewer words than linear notes.

Example 3:

These are some notes taken by someone who works at the Sports Club during a staff meeting.

Linear notes

Ideas for new leisure activities

       Inside the Sports Club

       – More aerobics classes

       – Yoga classes

       In the Sports Club grounds

       – Netball tournament

       – Five-a-side football

       Using other local facilities

       – Ask local hockey club for ideas

       – Offer roller skating lessons?

       – Ask local school about their race track

Web notes or Patterned notes

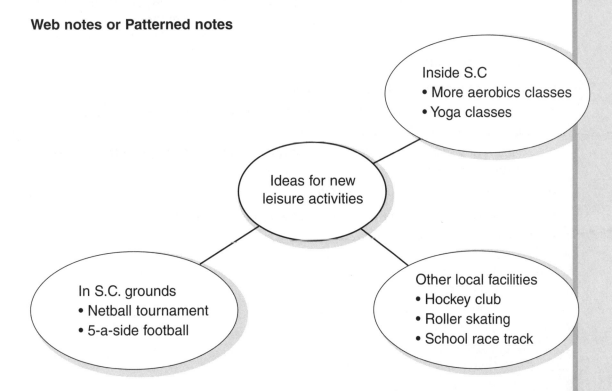

Exercise 9: Make some linear notes and web notes from the Sports Club advertising brochure at the beginning of this book.

Sample Assignment

Background

In Assignment 1 you began researching television soaps by conducting a survey. You are now asked to work on your own to find and use different research sources to investigate the topic further.

Tasks

1   Access the Internet, visit the library, ask your family, friends, teachers or anyone who might know where to find out information on the research topic from Assignment 1.

2   Find and read two documents about the research topic (one must include an image e.g. a chart that you can interpret).

3   Use a dictionary to help you understand any unfamiliar words.

4   Make copies of the documents.

5   Use a highlighter to mark out the key points on your copy of the documents.

6   Make summary notes of the two articles.

7   Find and read other articles on CD-ROM, newspapers, magazines etc. about the research topic – record the date of the article, the author etc.

Evidence to be collected

- Notes of research sources from task 1.

- Copies of your two chosen documents (remember one must include an image) with the key points highlighted.

- Notes of words that you looked up in a dictionary and what you found their meanings to be.

- Summary notes of the two articles.

- Notes of other articles you have found on the subject for task 7.

Relating the assignment to the specification

Specification Reference (Part B)	What has been done to satisfy this
C1.1	
• Provide information that is relevant to the subject and purpose of the discussion.	
• Speak clearly in a way that suits the situation.	
• Listen and respond appropriately to what others say.	
C1.2	
• Read the relevant material.	• Tasks 1, 2, 3 and 7
• Identify accurately the main points and ideas in material.	• Tasks 5 and 6
• Use the information to suit your purpose.	• Tasks 5 and 6
C1.3	
• Present relevant information in a form that suits your purpose.	
• Ensure text is legible.	
• Make sure that spelling, punctuation and grammar are accurate so your meaning is clear.	

Other Key Skills signposting

Information Technology IT1.1 if you use an IT information source.

Ideas for other assignments

- A research topic from your main area of study.

- Research on your home town.

- Research about one of your favourite charities.

Sample test questions

Questions 1 - 6 are based on the following article that appeared in a local newspaper recently.

East Anglian property prices
Riding high over the decade

A new survey published today will show that property prices in East Anglia have almost doubled over the past decade.

For example, omitted from the table are towns like Wisbech, which saw an average rise of just 48%. Economists warn that the

Average Property Prices

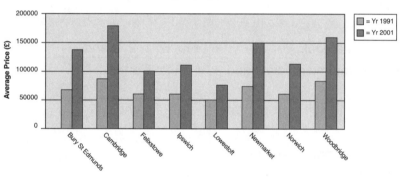

The Halifax - the UK's largest mortgage lender, compiled this study of house values. It finds that house prices in East Anglia have risen by an average 88% over the past decade, compared with a national average of 75%. However, the average figure of 88% does mask huge variations across the region.

prospect of rising unemployment and higher interest rates later in the year would begin to constrain the market.
Overall, house price growth in this region is forecast to slow to about 3% this year, below the UK average of 5%.

---

1   This article is formatted into:

   A   tables

   B   words

   C   columns

   D   rows

2   Which of the following statements is correct?

   A   property prices have almost tripled over the past 10 years

   B   property prices have gone down over the past 10 years

   C   property prices have stayed the same over the past 10 years

   D   property prices have almost doubled over the past 10 years

3   One reason price rises might slow down in the future is because:

    A   people will not want to buy houses

    B   unemployment will rise

    C   there will be too many houses

    D   house prices will be too cheap

4   What was the average price rise in Wisbech?

    A   48%

    B   75%

    C   88%

    D   5%

5   Which of the following statements is correct for 2001?

    A   the average price of a house is higher in Woodbridge than in Lowestoft

    B   the average price of a house is higher in Ipswich than in Newmarket

    C   the average price of a house is higher in Felixstowe than in Cambridge

    D   the average price of a house is higher in Norwich than in Newmarket

6   Which of the following statements is NOT correct?

    A   the average house price in Cambridge in 2001 was over £150,000

    B   the average house price in Ipswich in 2001 was less than £200,000

    C   the average house price in Ipswich in 1991 was over £200,000

    D   the average house price in Ipswich in 2001 was less than £150,000

Questions 7 – 11 are based on this job advertisement which appeared in a newspaper recently.

Senior Child Care Staff
Salary £15,610 to £18,450
+ sleep-in pay & pension

You should be an optimist with a good sense of humour and have experience at a senior level. A childcare qualification would be preferred.

The successful applicant will be required to run the youth club and sleep-in at the home two evenings per week. He or she will also help organise sporting activities one day every other weekend.

Closing date 18^h March   Interviews 27^h March

Please apply to:
Mrs K. King
Meresbrook Children's Home
Meresbrook
JK88 0LL

---

7   You need to send in an application for this job by:

A   27th March

B   18th March

C   18th May

D   tomorrow

8   The best way to apply for this job would be to:

A   write a letter

B   write a memo

C   write an essay

D   send a text message

9   The wage for this job is:

A   more than £20,000 per year

B   more than £15,000 per year

C   £27,000 per year

D   £2.50 per hour

10   Which of these would be most appropriate to include with your application letter?

A   a letter from your mum

B   a report

C   your school certificates

D   a CV

11 You should apply for this job if you:

  A are an experienced child care worker

  B are a school leaver

  C can only work during the day

  D cannot work weekends

Questions 12 – 14 are based on this flyer that was delivered to homes in the local area.

Headly Stables
Manure Supplies

- Well-rotted organic horse manure compost
- Supplied in large sealed bags
- Weed free
- Ideal for rosebeds, vegetable gardens and herbaceous borders

Call now – telephone 09987 9877892
For prompt service

12 What would be the best way to contact the stables for a delivery of manure?

  A write them a letter

  B visit the stables

  C send them a fax

  D telephone them

13 How is the manure supplied?

  A in wheelbarrows

  B in small carrier bags

  C in large sealed bags

  D in dustbins

Chapter 12
Writing Documents

Produce different types of document

These are some of the most common types of documents you are likely to have to write.

Writing letters

If you are writing a letter to a friend, you can be very informal and you do not have to follow any rules. However, if you are writing to someone you do not know in another organisation you need to write a more formal letter.

Ideally you should use a word processor to type this kind of letter. Remember that the letter you write gives an impression of you.

Try to structure the main body of your letter in the following way:

- **!** Part 1 – Introduce yourself and explain why you are writing.

- **!** Part 2 – Give details and supporting information. This may be spread over several paragraphs.

- **!** Part 3 – Say what you want to happen next.

The letter on the following page has been sent to the Sports Club manager. It shows how a letter should be laid out and the different things that should be included.

The style used is called **fully blocked** with **open punctuation** and it has a few simple rules for you to remember:

- **!** No punctuation until after the SUBJECT HEADING.

- **!** No punctuation after the full stop at the end of the last paragraph.

- **!** Normal use of punctuation in main body of the letter.

- **!** One blank line between paragraphs.

- **!** No indents at the beginning of lines.

YOUR ADDRESS → - you wouldn't need this if you are using headed notepaper	13 Acacia Avenue East Harling Essex CR5 8YH
REFERENCE → - this may have been given in the advertisement	Your ref: J05/01
DATE →	15th March 2001
READER'S NAME & ADDRESS →	Mr P Grey Manager Broomhill Sports Club Hale Road East Harling Essex CR8 9JK
SALUTATION → - the greeting	Dear Mr Grey
SUBJECT HEADING → - a summary of the letter	**Part-time Sports Assistant**
BODY OF LETTER →	I am writing in response to your advertisement that appeared in the Essex Daily Times recently for the above post. I am currently a second year student at Essex College studying for a National Diploma in Sports Studies. As I hope to find employment in the sports/leisure industry when I leave college I need to gain some practical experience to back up the more theoretical aspects we are covering on the course. The position you advertised sounds ideal for someone like myself who is quite willing to work outside normal hours. I am a hard-working, enthusiastic individual who can work independently or as part of a team as I communicate well with others. I enclose a CV which details my qualifications and work experience to date. It also mentions my leisure interests which as you can see centre mainly around a number of different sporting activities. I hope to have the opportunity of meeting you at an interview to discuss this opportunity in more detail.
COMPLIMENTARY CLOSE → - use **Yours faithfully** if you do not know their name	Yours sincerely
SIGNATORY → - the name of the person signing the letter	Shelley Shearman
ENCLOSURE → - this abbreviation is only used if you're enclosing something else in the envelope e.g. a CV	Enc

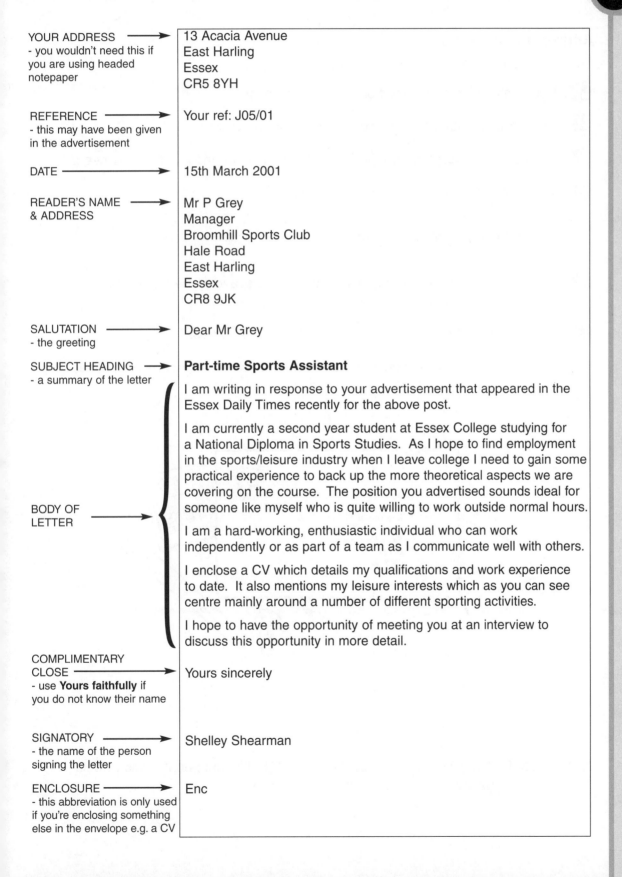

Chapter 12
Writing Documents

Addressing envelopes

There are several ways to address an envelope:

- Use printed labels produced on a word processor.

- Print straight onto the envelopes using a word processor.

- Use window envelopes through which the address on the letter can be seen.

- Write the address on the envelopes by hand.

Whichever method you are going to use, there are a few rules:

- Start about halfway down the envelope to leave space at the top for the stamp and postmark.

- The postcode should always be the last line in the address.

- Do not use any punctuation in the address and do not indent any of the lines.

Mr P Grey
Manager
Broomhill Sports Club
Hale Road
East Harling
Essex
CR8 9JK

Exercise 1: If you were sending out letters to 100 different people which would be the best way to address the envelopes?

Memos

A memo is written confirmation of a message. The word 'memo' is short for 'memorandum', which means 'note'.

Memos are normally sent internally within an organisation and can be quite informal documents.

The style used in the following example is called **fully blocked** with **open punctuation** and it has a few simple rules for you to remember:

! There is no salutation

! There is no complimentary close

! They do not normally require an envelope

! It is good practice to sign a memo

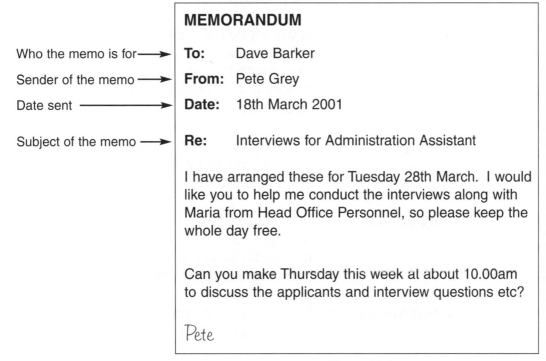

Who the memo is for ——►

Sender of the memo ——►

Date sent ——————►

Subject of the memo ——►

MEMORANDUM

To: Dave Barker

From: Pete Grey

Date: 18th March 2001

Re: Interviews for Administration Assistant

I have arranged these for Tuesday 28th March. I would like you to help me conduct the interviews along with Maria from Head Office Personnel, so please keep the whole day free.

Can you make Thursday this week at about 10.00am to discuss the applicants and interview questions etc?

Pete

Figure 12.2

Exercise 2: Dave Barker is due at Head Office for a meeting on the day his manager has arranged the interviews. Write a memo in reply from Dave Barker to Pete Grey.

Chapter 12
Writing Documents

Writing reports

Reports are practical documents. They are often a record of work that has been done, observations that have been made or recommendations for actions that should be taken in the future.

A manager may ask a member of staff to write a report that may be used as a basis for making decisions. This means that the report should be objective and present all the facts in a logical order so that valid conclusions can be drawn.

A sample structure for a report is shown below.

Objective means factual and not influenced by your own personal feelings. The opposite of objective is **subjective.** E.g. the following statement is objective: The coat is dark blue. The following statement is subjective: The coat is a lovely shade of blue.

A report summarising the usage of facilities at Broomhill Sports Club

Title	As above
Terms of reference	e.g. The following report aims to evaluate the current use of Sports Club facilities.
Methods	A description of the methods of research you used to enable you to to produce the report e.g. surveys, observations, interviews with people etc.
Findings	This section should describe your findings.You might include a table or chart to support your comments.
Conclusions	This section should summarise the data you collected. It should allow the reader to see which are the most important issues raised.
Recommendations	Only make recommendations if you've been asked to.
Signature & date	

Figure 12.3

Exercise 3: Look back at the spreadsheet shown in Figure 5.6 and suggest some content that could be written in the different sections of the above report.

Filling in forms

Most of us have to complete forms now and again during our everyday life. Some of the forms are simple – they just need basic information such as name, address and telephone number. Examples of simple forms include an application for a library ticket, a competition entry form, postal redirection form, electoral roll form, etc.

At times you are asked to complete a more complex form which requires more detailed information and longer answers. Examples of more complex forms include a job application form, accident report form, passport application, an income tax return form, etc.

Tips for filling in forms

- ! Don't rush it – allow enough time to do it carefully.

- ! Write neatly. Check to see how much space you have got so that you can adjust the size of your writing.

- ! Read through the form and make sure you understand all the words. If you don't, ask someone or look them up in a dictionary.

- ! Make sure you answer every question.

- ! Collect together any documents or information that you have to include with the form.

- ! Write in pencil first, then go over it in pen when you are sure it is correct (rubbing out the pencil).

- ! Read through the completed form to check it and then ask someone else to check what you have written.

- ! Write N/A next to any questions that do not apply to you.

- ! Make a copy of the completed form and keep it safe.

Tip:
Most forms require a signature. Make sure that yours is sensible and that it is roughly the same every time you use it.

Tip:
N/A stands for Not Applicable.

Understanding common words used on forms

It is much easier to fill in forms if you understand all the words. Here are some of the words you will often find.

Word	Meaning
Employment	Work
Forename	First name
Location	Place
Maiden name	A woman's surname before marriage
Marital status	Whether married, single, widowed, etc.
Next of kin	Nearest relative
Occupation	Type of work
Place of residence	Home address
Previous	One(s) before e.g. previous address
Qualifications	Exams passed or certificates gained
Referee	Person who will give you a reference
Remuneration	The amount you earn(ed)
Surname	Your last name or family name

Figure 12.4

Tip:

A **reference** is written by a previous employer, or someone who knows you well. It says how reliable and able you are.

Example 1:

Application for the post of _____

At _____

Surname _____

(Mr/Mrs/Miss/Ms) Delete where not applicable

Forenames _____

Maiden name (where applicable) _____

Date of birth _____

Address _____

_____

Postcode _____ Telephone No. _____

Qualifications

Title (e.g. GCSE)	Grade	Date

Are you registered under the Disabled Persons Act?   YES/NO

If yes, please give registration number _____

Current and Previous Employment

Please give details of your current and previous employment, starting with the most recent

Position	Employer's name & address	Date started	Date finished

---

Figure 12.5

Exercise 4: Complete the application form above for a job as Administration Assistant at Broomhill Sports Club.

Other types of document

Although you may not have to produce these documents, you should know the purpose of them and recognise their standard layouts.

Fax header sheets

Fax (short for 'facsimile') is extensively used by organisations. It has the great advantage that you can transmit hand-written documents or drawings and they arrive instantly at the other end. In addition to speed, the main advantage of faxing information is that a copy of the original document including any hand-written or drawn details is sent.

BROOMHILL
SPORTS CLUB

Fax

To:	East Harling Gazette	From:	D. Barker
Fax:	01789 2345	**Pages:**	2
Phone:	01789 1223	**Date:**	4/8/2002
Re:	Advertisement	**CC:**	

☐ **Urgent**   ☐ **For Review**   ☐ **Please Comment**   ☐ **Please Reply**   ☐ **Please Recycle**

Further to our recent telephone conversation please find attached the draft advertisement that we would like to place in the Entertainments section this Friday.

Let me know if you require any further details.

Many Thanks

Dave Barker

Figure 12.6

Exercise 5: Can you think of any disadvantages of faxed messages?

Agendas

An agenda is a document that is used to inform people of the date and time of a forthcoming meeting, the topics for discussion and the order in which topics will be discussed. The person who is going to chair the meeting normally produces the agenda.

BR⊙⊙MHILL
SPORTS CLUB

The next staff meeting will take place on Monday, 9th January, at 13.30 in the Meeting Room.

Agenda

1. Apologies for absence.

2. Minutes of last meeting (please make sure you have these with you).

3. Matters arising from minutes.

4. Manager's report.

5. Advertising.

6. Staffing rota.

7. New fitness reviews.

8. Customer comments.

9. Any other business.

10. Date of next meeting.

Figure 12.7

Minutes

The secretary of the meeting keeps the minutes – sometimes a specific minutes secretary is elected. He or she records all the matters that were discussed at the meeting, any decisions that were made and any actions that result, noting what is to be done and by whom.

BROOMHILL
SPORTS CLUB

Minutes of the staff meeting held on Monday 9th January 2002.

Present: Pete Grey (Chair), Dave Barker (Secretary), Shelley Shearman, Doug King, Ali Raymond, Imran Howes.

Apologies for absence were received from Victor Dew.

1. **MINUTES OF THE LAST MEETING**
   The minutes of the last meeting were agreed.

2. **MATTERS ARISING**
   None.

3. **MANAGER'S REPORT**
   Pete Grey presented the Health Club revenue figures for the past three months. The meeting discussed these figures and what could be done to improve them.
   ACTION: Pete Grey

4. **ADVERTISING**
   The content of the advertising posters was agreed. It was decided to place an advertisement in the local paper.
   ACTION: Dave Barker

5. **STAFFING ROTA**
   This is to become the responsibility of Shelley, who will produce a new format for the rota.
   ACTION: Shelley Shearman

6. **NEW FITNESS REVIEWS**
   All members are to be offered the new-style fitness review. A flyer will be produced.
   ACTION: Dave Barker

7. **CUSTOMER COMMENTS**
   No comments have been received for discussion

8. **ANY OTHER BUSINESS**
   None.

9. **DATE OF NEXT MEETING**
   April 16th 2002 at 13.30.

Figure 12.8

Invoices

Invoices are used to request payment from customers for goods or services.

Hale Road
East Harling
Essex
CR5 8YH

INVOICE

Invoice No. INV10433

Invoice Address		Delivery Address			
St. Lewis School 58B Long Lane Ipswich Suffolk IP8 7UI					

Date	Order Date	Account No.	Our Order No.	Customer Ref.	Contact
31/1/02	31/12/01	D030	ORD09427		Jane Green

Qty	Description		Unit Price	Value
1	Hire of soft play area		135.00	135.00
20	Sandwich lunch		1.50	30.00
			VAT	28.88
Payment 30 days from invoice date			**Total**	**193.88**

Figure 12.9

Spell words correctly

It is easy to spoil a piece of written work with poor spelling. Some people will not take what you have written seriously if you haven't spelt it correctly.

! Always use a dictionary if you are unsure of a spelling.

! Use a spell-checker if you are working on a computer (see Chapter 4).

There are some rules of spelling that you should try to remember and some words that sound similar but have different spellings.

Vowels

The vowels are **A E I O U.** There is a spelling rule for these that nearly always works: **'I before E except after C'**

e.g. thief, believe and grieve but receive, deceive and perceive.

Consonants

Consonants are all the letters of the alphabet that are not vowels.

Plurals

The most common plural form is to add an 's' to the word.

e.g. books, names, machines etc.

If the singular word ends in 'sh', 'ch', 'ss', 's', 'x', or 'z' then add 'es'.

e.g. washes, churches, masses, boxes, fizzes etc.

If the singular word ends in 'y', then change the 'y' to 'ies'.

e.g. dairies, parties, marries etc.

but when the 'y' follows a vowel, this rule does not apply.

e.g. boys, days etc.

But some words just break all the rules!

e.g. women, children, sheep etc.

Exercise 6: Write down the plurals of the following words

computer

lamp

daisy

worry

desk

pie

key

patio

journey

Prefixes

Prefixes are added to the front of words to change their meaning.

Here are some examples:

Prefix	Meaning	Examples
anti-	against or opposite to	anticlockwise, anticlimax
dis-	not, or away	disinfect, dissimilar, disconnect
il-	not	illogical, illegal
im-	not	immature, improbable
in-	not	insane, indistinct
inter-	between	international, interval
ir-	not	irrelevant, irregular
mis-	wrong	misunderstand, misspell
post-	after	postnatal, postscript
pre-	before	prejudge, prehistoric
pro-	for, or forward	propose, progress
re-	again, or back	reword, reconsider
sub-	under	submarine, substandard
super-	above	supervisor, superhuman
trans-	across	transport, transplant
un-	not, or in reverse	unfinished, unknown

Exercise 7: Complete the following table, adding the appropriate prefixes.

Not possible		**Not** perfect	
Not logical		**Across** the world	
After war		**Not** literate	

Chapter 12
Writing Documents

Communication **3**

Suffixes

Suffixes are added to the end of words to change their meaning.

Here are some (but there are lots more!). You will see that sometimes the base word changes when you add a suffix.

Suffixes	Examples
-ful	hopeful, thankful
-less	useless, tasteless
-let	booklet, pamphlet
-ly	bravely, ideally
-ment	movement, agreement
-ness	loveliness, happiness
-er, -or	baker, collector
-en	stolen, hidden
-ish	foolish, thinnish
-ation	automation, reservation
-ing	sitting, knitting
-ity	scarcity, hilarity
-y	noisy, tasty

Here are a few tips about suffixes that might help with spelling:

If you add a suffix to a short word that has a vowel before a single consonant at the end of the word, then double the consonant. e.g. fitter, fittest, bigger, biggest etc.

Words where the final consonant is followed by an 'e', drop the 'e' when a suffix is added. e.g. living, having, giving etc.

Exercise 8: See if you can complete the table below:

Base word	Suffix	New word
Interest	-ing	
Hope	-less	
Excite	-ing	
Swede	-ish	
Control	-er	
Plan	-ing	

Words that sound the same

Words that sound the same but are spelt differently are called **homophones**. Many people get confused about which word to use when.

Word	Meaning or use	Example
There	To do with a place	The book is over there
Their	Belonging to them	The children read their books
They're	Used to shorten they are	They're really enjoying it
To	Used to describe an action	I went to the library
Too	Used when there is too much of something or used to mean as well	I was far too cold It was cold and it was raining too
Two	Used when writing the number 2	There were two books on the shelf
It's	Used to shorten it is	It's cold today
Its	Used to describe something belonging to something	The office was hot because all its windows were shut.
Here	Used to write about where places or things are	The door key is here
Hear	Used to describe listening	Can you hear the music?

Exercise 9: Which of these sentences are correct?

Please come over hear and show me your book.

Its no good trying to make excuses.

I was feeling very tired two.

I think I will sit over there.

Some boys played they're music really loudly.

I would love to here about your holiday.

They're too young to see that film.

Grammar

There are lots of rules of grammar – this means putting sentences together properly. If you can get some of these rules straight it will help you to communicate well with other people.

The different parts of speech have different names. Two of the most important are:

 The **subject** of the sentence. This is who or what is being talked or written about. For example I, he/she/it, we, you, they, Jack or the dog.

 The **verb** in the sentence. These are 'doing' words. For example to speak, to send, to run etc.

It is important to get the **tense** of a verb correct. The tense of a verb tells us something about the time period we are talking about e.g. the past, the present or the future. You must not jump between the past, present and future in a piece of writing because it can be very confusing for the reader.

You also have to be careful to match the verb with the subject.

You must remember that singular subjects take 's' verbs and plural subjects take no 's' verbs. For example:

The man delivers
The men deliver

The woman talks
The women talk

An important exception to this rule is the verb 'to be'

Past	Present	Future
I was	I am	I will be *or* I shall be
You were	You are	You will be
She was	She is	She will be
We were	We are	We will be *or* We shall be
They were	They are	They will be

Punctuation

Punctuation helps your writing make sense. Sentences always start with a capital letter and end with a full stop. Longer pieces of written work should be organised into paragraphs.

Paragraphs always start on a new line, sometimes with an indent at the beginning of the line. They indicate a different section of the writing.

Here are some common punctuation marks that you need to be able to use.

Name of punctuation mark	Symbol	Function
Full stop	.	Ends a sentence
Comma	,	Indicates a pause or separates items in a list
Question mark	?	Indicates a question
Exclamation mark	!	Indicates surprise or emphasises a point
Quotation marks	" Hello "	Encloses speech or a quotation
Apostrophe	'	Indicates ownership (e.g. the boy's pen) or indicates omission (e.g. don't do that)

Chapter 12
Writing Documents

Using apostrophes

The apostrophe is used for two main reasons in the English language:

1   To show that one or more letters are missing, for example:

They've really enjoyed themselves today – the apostrophe shows that **ha** is missing from **They have.**

2   To show ownership, for example:

For singular words add **'s**

This is Jane's room – the room belongs to Jane so the apostrophe goes after Jane.

Note that even if the word ends in an **s**, still add an **'s** to the end e.g. Charles's room.

For plural words add **'s**

This is the children's room – the room belongs to the children so the apostrophe goes after children.

Note that if the word ends in an **s**, just add ' (apostrophe alone) to the end e.g. This is the teachers' room.

Exercise 10: Punctuate the following sentences with apostrophes according to the rules given above.

1   Its important that you know the basic rules of First Aid.

2   Whos going to the party tomorrow?

3   I have three books and Mikes got five.

4   Didnt you know theyre moving out tomorrow?

5   Its a sunny day so Ive decided to wear my sunglasses.

6   The Jones children are playing outside.

7   The invoice showed £50 as its total.

8   Yours is the table over there.

Proof-reading

You should always proof-read your work before you hand it in. This applies to hand-written work and work that you have produced on the computer and which you have checked with the spelling and grammar check.

Sometimes it can be difficult proof-reading your own work – you see what you want to see and end up not spotting all the mistakes.

The problems could be:

! Spelling

! Punctuation – especially mistakes with apostrophes, using commas instead of full stops and forgetting capital letters at the beginning of sentences.

! Using the wrong word like the homophones we looked at earlier.

Here are some tips for proof-reading:

▶ If it is possible, read your work out aloud. This makes you read it slower and you are more likely to spot mistakes.

▶ If you're not sure of which word to use or how to spell it, ask someone who does know or look it up in a dictionary.

▶ Keep a particular lookout for things you often get wrong – most people have a few words that they are never sure how to spell – you are not alone!

▶ If you tend to leave out apostrophes, check every word that ends in –s to see if it needs an apostrophe. If you tend to put in too many apostrophes, check every apostrophe to see if you can justify it with a rule for using apostrophes.

▶ Ask someone else to read through your work for you.

Exercise 11: On the following page is the original text that was produced for the Broomhill brochure before it was proof-read. Make a note of all the errors you can find.

BROOMHILL SPORTS CLUB

Fitness for all

Get in shape with us!   A new approach to a healthy lifestyle
We offer you more than you expect:

- A choice of over 30 activities
- Trayned instructors available
- All inclusive membership or 'pay as you go'
- Luxury changing Facilities
- Free members magazine
- Health and Beauty
- All facilities and services FREE to members'

SWIMMING
Our 20m swimming pool have allocated speed lanes at all times.
Adults: £1.80 per hour   Children: £110 per hour

ARCHERY
Why not try artchery lessons with our qualified instructor
Tues and Thurs: 10.00 – 11.00am   £3.50 per person.
Must be booked in advance.

FOOTBALL
Football is not just for the men – we have women and girls teams as well as boys and men competing in local leagues at all levels.
Ask reception for details.

SQUASH
Book one of our three squash court and join the squash 'ladder'
£3.50 per court, per hour.

AEROBICS
Our aerobic classes are very popular – work out with your friends.
Every morning 9.30 – 10.30am £2.50 per person.

TENNIS
Broomhill boasts too indoor courts in addition to four outdoor ones.
£2.50 per person per court.

GYMNASIUM
We have a fully equipped gymnasium with all of the latest equipment.
£2.50 per hour Over 16s only.

OTHER SPORTS
Many other activities is available including basketball, badmington and table tennis.
All activities Free to members

Well help you achieve a better lifestyle.
Look better! Feel better Work better! Sleep better!

Sample Assignment

Background

Your research into television soaps for Assignments 1 and 2 should now be complete. You must now work individually to write two documents related to the research.

Tasks

1   The first document should be a report based on the group survey results and the information you found and read in Assignment 2.

    •   Ideally the report should be word-processed with subheadings to organise different sections.

    •   Spell-check and proof-read the document before handing it in.

    •   The report that you produce should include an appropriate and relevant image that you refer to and explain its purpose.

2   The second document should be a questionnaire for the survey that you conducted in Assignment 1. Whilst conducting the interview in Assignment 1 you asked the questions and noted down the answers. Assume now you need a professional-looking questionnaire that you are going to hand out to interviewees for them to complete. Ideally it should be word-processed, but if this is not possible then lay it out neatly by hand.

The questions should be:

    •   easy to understand

    •   in a standard format

    •   easy to answer (multiple-choice/tick boxes where appropriate)

    •   spaced out sensibly (i.e. with enough space for a written response)

Evidence to be collected

•   Drafts of the two documents annotated by hand with corrections.
•   The final two documents (remember one must include an appropriate image).

Relating the assignment to the specification

Specification Reference (Part B)	What has been done to satisfy this
C1.1	
• Provide information that is relevant to the subject and purpose of the discussion.	
• Speak clearly in a way that suits the situation.	
• Listen and respond appropriately to what others say.	
C1.2	
• Read the relevant material.	
• Identify accurately the main points and ideas in material.	
• Use the information to suit your purpose.	
C1.3	
• Present relevant information in a form that suits your purpose.	• Tasks 1 and 2
• Ensure text is legible.	• Tasks 1 and 2
• Make sure that spelling, punctuation and grammar are accurate so your meaning is clear.	• Tasks 1 and 2

Other Key Skills signposting

Information Technology IT1.2

Application of Number N1.3

Ideas for other assignments

! A report on a research topic for your main area of study.

! Standard business documents for a new company (e.g. letter, memo, fax header page, agenda and minutes).

! A letter of application for a job, together with a C.V.

! Promotional material for a new nightclub (e.g. flyer and poster).

Sample test questions

1   Which of the following sentences is spelt correctly?

    A   Sharon and Bob where too late.

    B   Sharon was not sure were she had left the video.

    C   Sharon and Bob went to return there video to the rental shop.

    D   When Sharon and Bob took their video back the shop was closed.

2   Which of the following sentences does not contain a grammatical error?

    A   I was waiting while my brother was looking for her jacket.

    B   Kay and Joe was very busy yesterday.

    C   The teacher gave out the book's to children in the class.

    D   She were really naughty last week.

Questions 3 - 6 are based on the letter in the box below written by Lesley Jacobs to the headmaster of her son's school.

She was rather rushed as she had to produce the letter on the computer before Nigel left for school, and a few spelling and grammatical errors crept in (underlined).

> 26 The Avenue
> Thurlsby
> Suffolk
> IP99 66 V
>
> Mr H James
> Headmaster
> Thurlsby High School
> Thurlsby Lane
> Thurlsby
> IP99 66 Z
>
> 12 February 2002
>
> Dear Mr James
>
> I <u>are</u> writing to inform you that my son Nigel will be absent from school on Tuesday. This is because he <u>had</u> a dental appointment in the morning. He is having several teeth extracted and will need the afternoon <u>too</u> recover.
>
> I <u>will</u> be grateful if you could help him to catch up with any work he misses that day.
>
> Yours sincerely
>
> Lesley Jacobs

3   In line 1 Lesley should have written:

    A   I am

    B   I is

    C   I were

    D   I maybe

4 In line 2 Lesley should have written:

A he will be having

B he were

C he is having

D he has

5 In line 4 instead of 'will' Lesley should have written:

A could

B would

C might

D won't

6 In line 3 Lesley should have written:

A to

B two

C 2

D for

7 Making sure information is correct before printing a final copy is known as:

A proof-reading

B security

C spell-checking

D backing up

8 Which of these documents is used to inform people of the date and time of a forthcoming meeting and the topics for discussion?

A Minutes

B Report

C Essay

D Agenda

9 On an application form which of these would be a correct entry for **Occupation**?

A Manchester

B Accountant

C Female

D £15,000

10 Which of these statements is true?

A Memos are normally sent to customers

B Memos must be more than one page long

C Memos are usually quite informal documents

D Memos should always be sent in large envelopes

> **COMMENTS ABOUT BOOKS**
> 1. The book was really good.
> 2. I suppose the library will have a copy of the book.
> 3. I'm sure you would enjoy the book.
> 4. The book was written by H. J. Lear.

11 Marita wants to find a good novel to read and asks a friend for advice. Which of the sentences in the box above is a fact and NOT an opinion?

A   1

B   2

C   3

D   4

12 Which of these statements describes a **prefix**?

A   letters added to the front of words to change their meaning

B   letters added to the end of words to change their meaning

C   letters added to the middle of words to change their meaning

D   vowels

13 If you are writing to Mr Timpson at the bank, you would close the letter with:

A   Yours faithfully

B   See you!

C   Lots of love

D   Yours sincerely

14 Which of these is spelt correctly?

A   disappear

B   dissappear

C   dissapear

D   disapear

15 If you had to send an urgent document that included a signature, how would you send it?

A   by telephone

B   by a text message on a mobile phone

C   by fax

D   by e-mail

16 Which of these statements is true?

A   sentences generally start with a capital letter and end with a comma

B   sentences generally start with a capital letter and end with a full stop

C   sentences are generally over a page in length

D   sentences start with a lower case character and end with a full stop

Appendix A

QCA Specifications for Level 1

Appendix A
IT Level 1

Part A WHAT YOU NEED TO KNOW

In finding and developing information,

YOU NEED TO KNOW HOW TO:

- find different types of information *(eg text, images, numbers)* from IT sources *(eg files, CD-ROM)* and non-IT sources *(eg hand-written notes, price lists, diagrams)*;
- decide what information is relevant for your purpose *(eg to answer questions from a customer, write a report, help solve a problem, make something)*;
- enter and bring in information *(eg copy and paste text, import clip-art images)*, using formats that help development *(eg consistent use of spaces, tabs and returns, format of numbers, graphic features such as line thickness and shading)*;
- explore information *(eg ask the right questions to find things out, try out alternatives)*;
- develop information in the form of text, images and numbers *(eg organise information, carry out calculations)*.

In presenting information,

YOU NEED TO KNOW HOW TO:

- use appropriate layouts for presenting different types of information, including text, images and numbers *(eg select screen displays or pages for different types of document, such as letters or invoices)*;
- present information in a consistent way *(eg fonts, bullet and number lists, alignments, size and position of images, tables of numbers)*;
- develop the presentation to meet your purpose *(eg organise the presentation by moving, copying, deleting and inserting information)*;
- make sure your work is accurate and clear *(eg check content is relevant, proof-read, use a spell-checker, ask others, select and highlight information to improve its clarity)*;
- save information so it can be found easily *(eg use suitable folders /directories, filenames)*.
- you will also need to know how IT can help you in your work and be able to compare your use of IT with other methods.
- it is important that you can work safely and take care of equipment, avoid losing information and know how to get help when dealing with errors.

Part B WHAT YOU MUST DO

You must:	Evidence must show you can:
IT1.1	
Find, explore and develop information for **two** different purposes.	• find and select relevant information; • enter and bring in information, using formats that help development; and • explore and develop information to meet your purpose.
IT1.2	
Present information for **two** different purposes. Your work must include at least **one** example of text, **one** example of images and **one** example of numbers.	• use appropriate layouts for presenting information in a consistent way; • develop the presentation so it is accurate, clear and meets your purpose; and • save information so it can be found easily.

Part C

Examples of activities you might use

You will have opportunities to develop and apply your IT skills during your work, studies or other activities.

For example, when:

- doing a project, or assignment, and presenting your findings;
- finding things out for customers or clients;
- exchanging information and ideas with work colleagues or other students.

You will need time to practise your skills and prepare for assessment. So it is important to plan ahead.

The purpose for using IT can be decided by you or by other people. But you must make sure that the work you produce suits this purpose. Using IT can contribute evidence of your use of other key skills, such as communication and application of number.

You will need to think about the quality of your IT skills and check your evidence covers all the requirements in Part B.

Examples of evidence

1.1 FIND AND DEVELOP INFORMATION

Print-outs and copies of the information you selected to use.

A record from an assessor who observed you using IT when exploring and developing information or working drafts with notes of how you met the requirements of the unit.

1.2 PRESENT INFORMATION

Working drafts showing how you developed the presentation or records from an assessor who saw your screen displays.

Print-outs or prints of a static or dynamic screen display of your final work, including examples of text, images and numbers.

Records of how you saved information.

If producing certain types of evidence creates difficulties, through disability or for another reason, you may be able to use other ways to show your achievement. Ask your tutor or supervisor for further information.

Application of Number Level 1

Part A WHAT YOU NEED TO KNOW

In interpreting information,

YOU NEED TO KNOW HOW TO:

- read and understand straightforward tables, charts, diagrams and line graphs;

- read and understand numbers used in different ways *(eg large numbers in figures or words, simple fractions, decimals, percentages)*;

- measure in everyday units *(eg minutes, millimetres, litres, grams, degrees)* by reading scales on familiar measuring equipment *(eg watch, tape measure, measuring jug, weighing scales, thermometer)*;

- make accurate observations *(eg count number of people or items)*;

- identify suitable calculations to get the results you need for your task.

In carrying out calculations,

YOU NEED TO KNOW HOW TO:

- work to the level of accuracy you have been told to use *(eg round to the nearest whole unit, nearest 10, two decimal places)*;

- add, subtract, multiply and divide with whole numbers and simple decimals *(eg two decimal places)*;

- understand and find simple fractions and percentages *(eg 2/3 of £15 is £10, 75% of 400 is 300)*;

- work out areas of rectangular spaces *(eg floor area)*;

- work out volumes of rectangular-based shapes *(eg a box)*;

- use straightforward scales on diagrams *(eg 10mm to 1m)*;

- use ratios and proportion *(eg three parts to one part)*;

- find the average (mean) of up to 10 items *(eg temperatures, prices, time)*;

- find the range for up to 10 items *(eg temperature range from highest to lowest was 16°C)*;

- check calculations using different methods *(eg estimate to reject impossible answers, check a subtraction by 'adding back')* to make sure they make sense.

In interpreting results and presenting your findings,

YOU NEED TO KNOW HOW TO:

- use suitable ways of presenting information, including a chart and diagram;

- use the correct units *(eg for area, volume, weight, time, temperature)*;

- label your work correctly *(eg use a title or key)*;

- describe how the results of your calculations meet the purpose of your task.

Part B WHAT YOU MUST DO

You must:	Evidence must show you can:
N1.1	
Interpret straightforward information from **two** different sources. At least **one** source should be a table, chart, diagram or line graph.	• obtain the information you need to meet the purpose of your task; and • identify suitable calculations to get the results you need.
N1.2	

Carry out straightforward calculations to do with:
      a. amounts and sizes;
      b. scales and proportion;
      c. handling statistics.
	• carry out calculations to the levels of accuracy you have been given; and
	• check your results make sense.

N1.3	
Interpret the results of your calculations and present your findings. You must use **one** chart and **one** diagram.	• choose suitable ways to present your findings; • present your findings clearly; and • describe how the results of your calculations meet the purpose of your task

Part C

Examples of activities you might use

You will have opportunities to develop and apply your number skills during your work, studies or other activities.

For example, when:

- carrying out an investigation, project or assignment;
- making something;
- helping customers or clients.

You will need time to practise your skills and prepare for assessment. So it is important to plan ahead.

You can obtain information first-hand by measuring or observing, but you do not have to do this.

Your information could come from written sources only. If available, you could use IT to present your findings, but you must show you understand what you have presented.

You will need to think about the quality of your work and check your evidence covers all the requirements in Part B.

Examples of evidence

1.1 INTERPRET INFORMATION

A description of your tasks and their purposes.

Copies of source material (such as a table, chart, diagram or line graph).

A statement from an assessor who checked the accuracy of your measurements or observations (if you have done this).

Records of the information you obtained and the types of calculations you identified to get the results you needed.

1.2 CARRY OUT CALCULATIONS

Records of your calculations (for a, b and c) and how you checked them.

1.3 INTERPRET RESULTS AND PRESENT FINDINGS

Descriptions of your findings and how the results of your calculations met the purposes of your tasks.

At least one chart and one diagram presenting your findings.

If producing certain types of evidence creates difficulties, through disability or for another reason, you may be able to use other ways to show your achievement. Ask your tutor or supervisor for further information.

Communication Level 1

Part A WHAT YOU NEED TO KNOW

In discussions,

YOU NEED TO KNOW HOW TO:

- find out about the subject so you can say things that are relevant;

- judge when to speak and how much to say;

- say things that suit the purpose of the discussion *(eg describe events, express opinions, develop ideas)*;

- speak clearly in a way that suits the situation *(eg use appropriate tone of voice, expressions and manner to suit the formality of the situation, use language that everyone can understand)*;

- show you are listening closely to what others say *(eg use body language, ask questions, make relevant comments, follow instructions, take messages)*.

In reading and obtaining information,

YOU NEED TO KNOW HOW TO:

- obtain advice from others on what to read for different purposes *(eg to get instructions, facts, opinions, ideas)*;

- identify the main points and ideas in different types of straight forward material *(eg letters, memos, extracts from books, newspaper or magazine articles)*, including images *(eg pictures, charts, diagrams, sketches)*;

- use a dictionary;

- ask others when you are unclear about what you have read;

- prepare information so it is suitable for use *(eg collate information as notes to use in discussions or written material such as a letter or short essay)*.

In writing documents,

YOU NEED TO KNOW HOW TO:

- use different written forms of presenting information *(eg business letters, memos, application forms, notes, short reports or essays)*;

- use images to help the reader understand your main points *(eg pictures, charts, diagrams, sketches)*;

- judge the relevance of information and the amount to include for your purpose *(eg to give or obtain facts, opinions, ideas)*;

- make your meaning clear by writing, proofreading and re-drafting documents so that:

  - words you use most often in your work or studies are spelled correctly;

  - sentences are formed correctly *(eg with subject–verb agreement such as 'she was' 'we were', with consistent use of tense)*;

  - sentences are marked by capital letters, full stops and question marks and organised into paragraphs where appropriate.

Part B WHAT YOU MUST DO

You must:	Evidence must show you can:
C1.1	
Take part in a **one-to-one** discussion and a **group** discussion about different, straightforward subjects.	• provide information that is relevant to the subject and purpose of the discussion; • speak clearly in a way that suits the situation; and • listen and respond appropriately to what others say.
C1.2	
Read and obtain information from **two** different types of documents about straightforward subjects, including at least **one** image.	• read the relevant material; • identify accurately the main points and ideas in material; and • use the information to suit your purpose
C1.3	
Write **two** different types of documents about straightforward subjects. Include at least **one** image in one of the documents.	• present relevant information in a form that suits your purpose; • ensure text is legible; and • make sure that spelling, punctuation and grammar are accurate so your meaning is clear.

Part C

Examples of activities you might use

You will have opportunities to develop and apply your communication skills during your studies, work or other activities.

For example, when:

- doing an investigation, project or assignment;
- helping customers or clients;
- exchanging information and ideas with work colleagues or other students.

You will need time to practise your skills and prepare for assessment. So it is important to plan ahead.

The information you obtain by reading can be used in your discussions and written work.

If available, you could use IT to produce written material and images, such as a chart.

You will need to think about the quality of your communication skills and check your evidence covers all the requirements in Part B.

Examples of evidence

1.1 DISCUSSIONS

Records from an assessor who observed each discussion and noted how you met the requirements of the unit, or an audio/video tape of the discussions.

1.2 READING

A record of what you read and why, including a note or copy of the image.

Notes, highlighted text or answers to questions about the material you read.

Records of how you have used this information eg in your discussions for C1.1 or writing for C1.3.

1.3 WRITING

Two different documents might include a letter, a short report or essay, with an image such as a chart or sketch.

If producing certain types of evidence creates difficulties, through disability or for another reason, you may be able to use other ways to show your achievement. Ask your tutor or supervisor for further information.

Appendix B

Sample
Documents

Sample Documents - Appendix B

INFORMATION TECHNOLOGY LEVEL 1
KEY SKILLS LOG BOOK
UNIT SUMMARY

Candidate name _____

COMPONENT		PORTFOLIO REFERENCE
IT1.1 • Find, explore and develop information for *two* different purposes.	**Purpose 1**	
	Purpose 2	
IT1.2 • Present information for *two* different purposes.	**Purpose 1**	
	Text	
	Images	
	Numbers	
Your evidence for IT1.2 must include at least *one* example of each of text, images and numbers.	**Purpose 2**	
	Text	
	Images	
	Numbers	

Assessor _____   **Candidate** _____

Date _____   **Date** _____

Page Number _____

Sample Documents - Appendix B

INFORMATION TECHNOLOGY LEVEL 1
KEY SKILLS LOG BOOK
COMPONENT SHEET (IT1.1)

Candidate name _____

IT1.1 • Find, explore and develop information for two different purposes.				
ASSESSMENT CRITERIA		HOW MET	Date	Assessor's initials
• Find and select relevant information.	Purpose 1			
	Purpose 2			
• Enter and bring in information, using formats that help development.	Purpose 1			
	Purpose 2			
• Explore and develop information to meet your purpose.	Purpose 1			
	Purpose 2			

Assessor _____   Candidate _____

Date _____   Date _____

Page Number _____

Sample Documents - Appendix B

INFORMATION TECHNOLOGY LEVEL 1
KEY SKILLS LOG BOOK
COMPONENT SHEET (IT1.2)

Candidate name _____

IT1.2 • Present information, for two different purposes				
ASSESSMENT CRITERIA		**HOW MET**	**Date**	**Assessor's initials**
• Use appropriate layouts for presenting information in a consistent way.	Purpose 1			
	Purpose 2			
• Develop the presentation so it is accurate, clear and meets your purposes.	Purpose 1			
	Purpose 2			
• Save information so it can be found easily.	Purpose 1			
	Purpose 2			

Assessor _____   Candidate _____

Date _____   Date _____

Page Number _____

Sample Documents - Appendix B

APPLICATION OF NUMBER LEVEL 1
KEY SKILLS LOG BOOK
UNIT SUMMARY

Candidate name _____

COMPONENT		PORTFOLIO REFERENCE
N1.1 • Interpret straightforward information from *two* different sources. At least *one* source should be a table, chart, diagram *or* line graph.	Source 1	
	Source 2	
N1.2 • Carry out straightforward calculations.	Amounts and sizes	
	Scales and proportion	
	Handling statistics	
N1.3 • Interpret the results of your calculations and present your findings. Your must use one chart and one diagram.	Chart	
	Diagram	

Assessor _____   Candidate _____

Date _____   Date _____

Candidate: Page Number _____

Sample Documents - Appendix B

APPLICATION OF NUMBER LEVEL 1
KEY SKILLS LOG BOOK
COMPONENT SHEET (N1.1)

Candidate name _____

N1.1 • Interpret straightforward information from *two* different sources. At least *one* source should be a table, chart, diagram *or* line graph.				
ASSESSMENT CRITERIA		**HOW MET**	**Date**	**Assessor's initials**
• Obtain information you need to meet the purpose of your task.	Source 1			
	Source 2			
• Identify suitable calculations to get the results you need.	Source 1			
	Source 2			

Assessor _____ **Candidate** _____

Date _____ **Date** _____

Page Number _____

Sample Documents - Appendix B

APPLICATION OF NUMBER LEVEL 1
KEY SKILLS LOG BOOK
COMPONENT SHEET (N1.2)

Candidate name _____

N1.2 • Carry out straightforward calculations.				
ASSESSMENT CRITERIA		HOW MET	Date	Assessor's initials
• Carry out calculations to the levels of accuracy you have been given.	Amounts and sizes			
	Scales and proportions			
	Handling statistics			
• Check your results make sense.	Amounts and sizes			
	Scales and proportions			
	Handling statistics			

Assessor _____ Candidate _____

Date _____ Date _____

Page Number _____

Sample Documents - Appendix B

APPLICATION OF NUMBER LEVEL 1
KEY SKILLS LOG BOOK
COMPONENT SHEET (N1.3)

Candidate name _____

N1.3 • Interpret the results of your calculations and present your findings. You must use one chart and one diagram.				
ASSESSMENT CRITERIA		**HOW MET**	**Date**	**Assessor's initials**
• Choose suitable ways to present your findings.	Chart			
	Diagram			
• Present your findings clearly.	Chart			
	Diagram			
• Describe how the results of your calculations meet the purpose of the task.	Chart			
	Diagram			

Assessor _____   Candidate _____

Date _____   Date _____

Page Number _____

Sample Documents - Appendix B

COMMUNICATION LEVEL 1
KEY SKILLS LOG BOOK
UNIT SUMMARY

Candidate name _____

COMPONENT		PORTFOLIO REFERENCE
C1.1 • Take part in a one-to-one discussion and a group discussion about different, straightforward subjects.	One-to-one	
	Group	
C1.2 • Read and obtain information from *two* different types of document about straightforward subjects. *One* of the documents should include at least one image.	Document type 1	
	Document type 2	
	Image	
C1.3 • Write *two* different types of document about straightforward subjects. At least one of the documents should include an image.	Document type 1	
	Document type 2	
	Image	

Assessor _____   Candidate _____

Date _____   Date _____

    Page Number _____

COMMUNICATION LEVEL 1

KEY SKILLS LOG BOOK
COMPONENT SHEET (C1.1)

Candidate name _____

C1.1 • Take part in a one-to-one discussion and a group discussion about different, straightforward subjects.				
ASSESSMENT CRITERIA		**HOW MET**	**Date**	**Assessor's initials**
• Provide information that is relevant to the subject and the discussion.	One-to-one			
	Group			
• Speak clearly in a way that suits the situation.	One-to-one			
	Group			
• Listen and respond appropriately to what others say.	One-to-one			
	Group			

Assessor _____   Candidate _____

Date _____   Date _____

Page Number _____

Sample Documents - Appendix B
COMMUNICATION LEVEL 1
KEY SKILLS LOG BOOK
COMPONENT SHEET (C1.2)

Candidate name _____

C1.2 • Read and obtain information from *two* different types of document about straightforward subjects. *One* of the documents should include at least *one* image.				
ASSESSMENT CRITERIA		**HOW MET**	**Date**	**Assessor's initials**
• Read relevant material	**Document type 1**			
	Document type 2			
• Identify accurately the main points and ideas in material.	**Document type 1**			
	Document type 2			
• Use the information to suit your purpose.	**Document type 1**			
	Document type 2			

Assessor _____   Candidate _____

Date _____   Date _____

Page Number _____

COMMUNICATION LEVEL 1
KEY SKILLS LOG BOOK
COMPONENT SHEET (C1.3)

Candidate name _____

C1.3 • Write *two* different types of document about straightforward subjects. At least *one* of the documents should include an image.				
ASSESSMENT CRITERIA		HOW MET	Date	Assessor's initials
• Present relevant information in a form that suits your purpose.	Document type 1			
	Document type 2			
• Ensure text is legible	Document type 1			
	Document type 2			
• Make sure that spelling, punctuation and grammar are accurate so your meaning is clear.	Document type 1			
	Document type 2			

Assessor _____   Candidate _____

Date _____   Date _____

Page Number _____

Sample Documents - Appendix B

INFORMATION TECHNOLOGY
INFORMATION SEEKING RECORD SHEET

Level _____

Candidate name _____ Date _____

Subject/Purpose _____

Information obtained	Source of information	How the search was made and the information selected

Attach printouts of information and notes of sources compared and used

Assessor _____ Candidate _____

Date _____ Date _____

Page Number _____

Sample Documents - Appendix B

INFORMATION TECHNOLOGY
WITNESS STATEMENT RECORD SHEET

Level _____

Candidate name _____ **Date** _____

Subject/Purpose _____

Task description

Assessor's comments

Assessor _____ **Candidate** _____

Date _____ **Date** _____

Page Number _____

Index